T0169154

The Hong Kong Economi

ON PRIVATIZING PUBLIC HOUSING

ON PRIVATIZING
PUBLIC HOUSING

Yue-Chim Richard Wong

Published for
The Hong Kong Centre for Economic Research
The Better Hong Kong Foundation
The Hong Kong Economic Policy Studies Forum
by

City University of Hong Kong Press

© 1998 by City University of Hong Kong Press

All rights reserved. No part of this publication may be reproduced,
stored in a retrieval system, or transmitted, in any form
or by any means, electronic, mechanical, photocopying,
recording, Internet or otherwise, without the prior written
permission of the City University of Hong Kong Press.

First published 1998
Printed in Hong Kong

ISBN 962-937-014-X

Published by
City University of Hong Kong Press
City University of Hong Kong
Tat Chee Avenue, Kowloon, Hong Kong

Internet: http://www.cityu.edu.hk/upress/
E-mail: upress@cityu.edu.hk

The free-style calligraphy on the cover, *gong*, means "public" in Chinese.

Contents

Detailed Chapter Contents

Foreword

The key to the economic success of Hong Kong has been a business and policy environment which is simple, predictable and transparent. Experience shows that prosperity results from policies that protect private property rights, maintain open and competitive markets, and limit the role of the government.

The rapid structural change of Hong Kong's economy in recent years has generated considerable debate over the proper role of economic policy in the future. The impending restoration of sovereignty over Hong Kong from Britain to China has further complicated the debate. Anxiety persists as to whether the pre-1997 business and policy environment of Hong Kong will continue.

During this period of economic and political transition in Hong Kong, various interested parties will be re-assessing Hong Kong's existing economic policies. Inevitably, some will advocate an agenda aimed at altering the present policy making framework to reshape the future course of public policy.

For this reason, it is of paramount importance for those familiar with economic affairs to reiterate the reasons behind the success of the economic system in the past, to identify what the challenges are for the future, to analyze and understand the economy sector by sector, and to develop appropriate policy solutions to achieve continued prosperity.

In a conversation with my colleague Y. F. Luk, we came upon the idea of inviting economists from universities in Hong Kong to take up the challenge of examining systematically the economic policy issues of Hong Kong. An expanding group of economists (The Hong Kong Economic Policy Studies Forum) met several times to give form and shape to our initial ideas. The Hong Kong Economic Policy Studies Project was then launched in 1996 with some 30 economists from the universities in Hong Kong and a few from overseas. This is the first time in Hong Kong history that a concerted public effort has been undertaken by academic economists in the territory. It represents a joint expression of our collective concerns, our hopes for a better Hong Kong, and our faith in the economic future.

The Hong Kong Centre for Economic Research is privileged to be co-ordinating this Project. We are particularly grateful to The Better Hong Kong Foundation whose support and assistance has made it possible for us to conduct the present study, the results of which are published in this monograph. We also thank the directors and editors of the City University of Hong Kong Press and The Commercial Press (H.K.) Ltd. for their enthusiasm and dedication which extends far beyond the call of duty. The unfailing support of many distinguished citizens in our endeavour and their words of encouragement are especially gratifying.

Yue-Chim Richard Wong
Director
The Hong Kong Centre
for Economic Research

Foreword by the Series Editor

Despite the common conception that the government plays a minimal role in economic affairs in Hong Kong, there are sectors where government intervention is very pronounced. The most prominent example is the housing market. Public housing in Hong Kong began in the early 1950s. As at end-1997, an estimated 34.4 per cent of the population lived in public-housing rental flats.

How did the Hong Kong government, with a well-recognized non-interventionist approach to the economy, ever get involved in the housing market? How has the government become engrossed in the provision of housing over time? Was it due to failure in the private market to cope with massive housing demand? How have public housing programmes developed and changed over the past few decades? How efficient have these programmes been in utilizing the vast amounts of resources they absorbed? Should the government continue to shoulder the responsibility of providing housing services to over one-third of the population?

This book addresses the above questions in detail. From the perspective of political economy, the book traces the history of government involvement in the housing market. It also points out the distortion and economic consequences of the public housing programme, and measures the benefits and costs of the programme to the tenants as well as to society as a whole.

The analysis discovers that for every dollar taxpayers spend on public housing, the tenants' enjoyment of the housing services amounts to only 59 cents in 1981 and 72 cents in 1991. In other words, some 41 and 28 per cent of the resources were wasted in the two years respectively. One manifestation of such inefficiency is the distortion of housing consumption by households. High-income households consume too little housing while low-income households consume too much. At the same time, there is no indication that the public housing programme has contributed to a more equitable distribution of income, a goal that the programme is supposed to reach.

In view of the gross amount of resource misallocation of the current public housing programme, the author, Professor Yue-chim Richard Wong proposes large-scale and rapid privatization of public housing. As a matter of fact, Professor Wong is one of the first proponents to privatize public housing and this book represents his summary view of such a proposal.

In December 1997 the Housing Authority also put forth its own proposal to sell public housing to the sitting tenants. Many issues remain to be resolved. The foremost issue is undoubtedly the pricing of public housing units. Other issues include the scope and pace of privatization, the resale of privatized units, the coordination of privatizing public housing with other government subsidized housing schemes, and so on. These issues are all discussed in detail and the differences between Professor Wong's proposal and that of the Housing Authority are highlighted.

Housing is probably the most discussed economic subject and the most concerned public policy issue in Hong Kong. The collapse of the private property market since late 1997 may confuse the issues underlying the privatization of public housing and even deter government action in that direction. However, the economic waste of the public housing programme has to be addressed whether the economy is in boom or in bust. Given Professor Wong's long-term interest and expertise in public housing, this book is a definite reference on the subject.

Y. F. Luk
School of Economics and Finance
The University of Hong Kong

Preface

I first became interested in the study of public housing in 1984, after the Housing Authority published a consultative document reviewing the policies of public housing allocation. I was drawn towards what appeared to me a highly inefficient and inequitable programme. Together with my colleague Professor Liu Pak Wai, I began to study the issues out of academic curiosity. The results of the study were subsequently published as the lead article in the *Journal of Urban Economics* in January 1988.

My interest in housing problems has been active for more than a decade, as policy issues regarding both housing and other matters continue to lead me back to the inefficiency and inequity of the public housing programme. I was convinced from the very beginning that privatization was the only solution to many of these problems. For over ten years, I have been promoting the idea to skeptics and opponents. Over time, they have grown more receptive or at least accustomed to my views. Perhaps my persistence has worn them down and they are tired of disagreeing, at least with me.

The failure of the initial privatization attempt in 1992 was a disappointment. Hong Kong and especially public housing tenants had to pay dearly for the failure as a result of the enormous inflation in property prices that took place in the following years. Privatizing public housing is now an official policy, after the Chief Executive of the Hong Kong Special Administrative Region government endorsed it in his first policy address to the Provisional Legislative Council on 8 October 1997. This is wonderful news for Hong Kong.

My research and thinking in this area owes a great deal to discussions with Professor Liu, Alan K. F. Siu, and also Tony Miller. I have also benefited from works published by Steven N. S. Cheung and Alan Smart. Many generations of assistants have contributed to this study in countless ways, and their unfailing commitment has finally borne fruit. I wish to acknowledge the help of Charmaine Lee, Lee Shuk-Fong, Sonia Wong Man-Lai, and Mon Ho Sau-Lan. The support of the Better Hong Kong Foundation is also greatly appreciated.

I would like to thank my family, whose understanding of my frequent absences and inability to meet domestic commitments has made it possible for me to complete this book. Jane, Michael, and Christina, I thank you from the bottom of my heart.

This book is dedicated to my mother and mother-in-law and to the memories of my father and father-in-law. As new immigrants to Hong Kong they experienced the harsh living conditions that Hong Kong offered in the post-war years. The sacrifices our parents endured have made it possible for our family to enjoy a fuller life.

Yue-Chim Richard Wong
School of Business and
School of Economics and Finance
The University of Hong Kong

List of Illustrations

Figures

Tables

On Privatizing Public Housing

CHAPTER 1

Introduction

Throughout Hong Kong's post-war history the government has intervened aggressively in the housing market. It has cleared vast squatter settlements that have appeared all over the territory. It has provided public housing directly to the population on a massive scale. The housing programme has evolved from one that provided resettlement units to squatters and low-cost rental units to lower income families to one that subsidizes home-ownership units marketed to middle-income households. The government has also imposed rent control on both pre-war and post-war private housing premises. These policies were often embarked upon without knowledge of what their consequences would be. They have affected the development of Hong Kong and the lives of ordinary residents in profound and often damaging ways.

From 1954 to 1996 Hong Kong's various public housing agencies built a total of 1,143,428 units. In 1996 over 3.1 million people, more than half of Hong Kong's population, lived in heavily subsidized government-provided housing. The rental discount on public housing units is about 80% of the market value, whereas the price discount on ownership units is about 50% of the market value. Naturally, there are long queues of people waiting eagerly to get into public housing units because of the generous subsidies that go along with them.

Table 1.1 contains data on various types of housing units produced by the public sector. One can see the historical evolution of the public programme in the changing composition of different types of housing units that were provided (Figures 1.1 and 1.2).

Table 1.1
Annual Production of Public Housing, 1954–97 and Forecasts to 2005

Year	RE (1)	FGLCH (2)	FHA (3)	NHA (4)	HOS (5)	PSPS (6)	MIH (7)	HS (8)	SWICH (9)	Total Produced (10)	Growth (%) (11)
1954 / 55	6,196									6,196	
1955 / 56	5,424							242		5,666	−9
1956 / 57	8,853							541		9,394	66
1957 / 58	5,557		1,955					270		7,782	−17
1958 / 59	6,988		638					968		8,594	10
1959 / 60	9,917		0					1,102		11,019	28
1960 / 61	11,285		2,845					898		15,028	36
1961 / 62	15,012		2,088					894		17,994	20
1962 / 63	15,063	1,246	3,953					1,600		21,862	21
1963 / 64	13,054	4,298	5,231					532		23,115	6
1964 / 65	23,106	4,984	4,505					3,826		36,421	58
1965 / 66	16,463	3,420	862					2,391		23,136	−36
1966 / 67	25,904	800	448					1,615		28,767	24
1967 / 68	22,006	4,832	1,331					2,054		30,223	5
1968 / 69	14,856	5,680	3,514					0		24,050	−20
1969 / 70	6,410	6,006	854					678		13,948	−42
1970 / 71	12,724	4,656	5,171					1,171		23,722	70
1971 / 72	6,495	12,612	1,472					916		21,495	−9
1972 / 73	6,776	12,912						0		19,688	−8
1973 / 74	1,970	6,200						325		8,495	−57
1974 / 75				9,200				586		9,786	15
1975 / 76				14,900				2,190		17,090	75
1976 / 77				9,620				486		10,106	−41
1977 / 78				13,020				504		13,524	34
1978 / 79				14,130				1,220		15,350	14
1979 / 80				29,759	2,439			800		32,998	115
1980 / 81				26,769	8,674	1,500		618		37,561	14
1981 / 82				31,346	4,399	0		3,725		39,470	5
1982 / 83				27,879	7,508	760		0		36,147	−8
1983 / 84				28,564	7,877	0	2,240	0		38,681	7
1984 / 85				26,354	10,168	1,408		354		38,284	−1
1985 / 86				29,386	6,688	11,902		116		48,092	26
1986 / 87				30,237	6,838	4,866		1,391		43,332	−10
1987 / 88				24,016	6,240	1,932		413		32,601	−25
1988 / 89				29,434	7,420	8,012		298		45,164	39
1989 / 90				45,044	10,922	6,450		795		63,211	40
1990 / 91				32,619	9,958	5,940		2,797		51,314	−19
1991 / 92				21,190	1,375	5,270		1,294		29,129	−43
1992 / 93				22,576	12,685	11,433		284		46,978	61
1993 / 94				19,848	10,592	1,960		426		32,826	−30
1994 / 95				24,440	10,477	2,297		0		37,214	13
1995 / 96				14,559	14,868	4,460		269	1,024	35,180	−5
1996 / 97*				14,946	13,188	3,690		971	0	32,795	−7
1997 / 98*				32,200		1,800		4,300	4,000	42,300	29
1998 / 99*				20,900		12,900		0	5,400	39,200	−7
1999 / 2000*				51,200		7,700		0	1,100	60,000	53
2000 / 01*				93,400		23,000		1,200	12,400	130,000	117
2001 / 02*				40,700		5,200		1,600	3,200	50,700	−61
2002 / 03*				42,500		5,000		4,600	3,200	55,300	9
2003 / 04*				45,000		6,300		0	10,000	61,300	11
2004 / 05*				37,300		11,000		0	10,000	58,300	−5

Source: Housing Authority, *Annual Report*, various issues; *Property Review*, various issues.

Notes: * Forecasted figures are obtained from the Housing Bureau. The Public-housing types are:
RE: resettlement estate, FGLCH: former Government Low Cost Housing, FHA: former Housing Authority, NHA: new Housing Authority, HOS: Home Ownership Scheme, PSPS: Private Sector Participation Scheme, MIH: middle-income housing, HS: Housing Society (rental), SWICH: sandwich class housing.

Figure 1.1
Annual Production of Public Housing, 1954–74

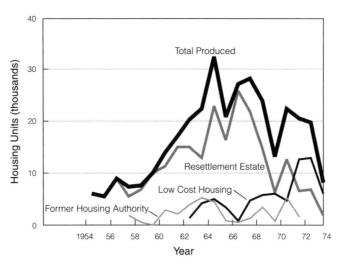

Source: Table 1.1, columns (1), (2), (3), (10).

Figure 1.2
Annual Production of Public Housing, 1974–97

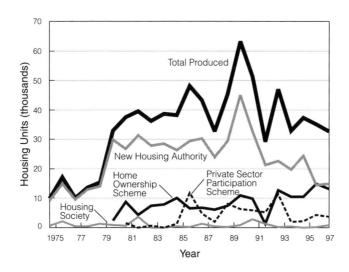

Source: Table 1.1, columns (4), (5), (6), (8), (10).

Figure 1.3
Annual Production of Public Housing, 1954–97 and Forecasts to 2005

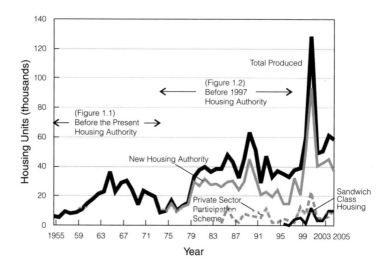

Source: Table 1.1, columns (4), (6), (9), (10).

According to the government's Long Term Housing Strategy Review published in January 1997, in the period 1995–96 to 2000–01 an additional 85,000 housing units will be required each year, of which 54,000 will be supplied by the public sector. For the period 2001–02 to 2005–06, a total of 73,000 units will be supplied each year, of which 39,000 will be from the public sector (Figure 1.3). These figures imply that the role of the public sector in housing will grow even more in the coming years. It represents a departure from proposals made since the 1980s in which it was envisioned that the public role will diminish. The main features of this new proposal has been reaffirmed in recent policy statements made by the government of the Special Administrative Region established on 1 July 1997.

Interpretations of the Origins of the Public Housing Programme

A great deal has been written about housing in Hong Kong and in particular about the massive public housing provision programme, which has been repeatedly identified as a "success story" (Castells, Goh, and Kwok 1990; Yeung and Drakakis-Smith 1982; Fung and Yeh 1987; Keung 1985). This literature is remarkably consistent, and analysts largely agree upon many points. Smart's (1992) work on squatter clearance is refreshingly penetrating and is the only obvious exception to the standard "success story" account. What is the conventional wisdom?

In brief, Hong Kong is seen as having faced a critical housing problem in the period after 1945. High levels of immigration from China, combined with destruction of the pre-war housing stock, resulted in overcrowding and the development of large squatter areas, wherein the impoverished refugees who could not afford private rents constructed their own makeshift dwellings. The housing shortage developed because the private sector could not profitably construct affordable housing for the large influx of low-income residents. These conditions created great problems for Hong Kong: threats to public health, large fires in squatter areas, the danger of riots, the barrier to development of the land which had been encroached upon by squatters, and the pressure on wages of high rents. Since the private sector was incapable of meeting the challenge, it was inevitable that the government would have to intervene, although this was postponed as long as possible because of the adherence to the philosophy of *laissez-faire* or positive non-interventionism (Smart 1992, pp. 5–6).

The public housing programme has therefore been hailed as a major achievement and as evidence of the positive aspects of government intervention to help the poor to gain access to decent housing that they could not otherwise afford (Yeh 1990). It has also been claimed that "the continuous flow of immigrants to Hong Kong that provided the basis of cheap labour for industrial growth could have generated an entire city of squatters if the public housing programme had not been there" (Castells, Goh, and Kwok 1990, p. 35).

The Welfare Argument

The specific reasons for why the government launched the squatter resettlement programme are still being disputed. Pryor (1983) sees the programme as an intervention on behalf and for the welfare of the residents of Hong Kong. In his view, it was instigated by the disastrous Shek Kip Mei squatter settlement fire on Christmas Day in 1953, which left 53,000 people homeless.

The Economic Argument

The economic interpretation of government intervention in the housing market appears in many studies. Denis Bray describes what happened on Boxing Day in 1953 when the governor Alexander Grantham made the decision to put the government into housing: "The resettlement programme of the fifties was not a housing programme for the poor. It was a means to clear land for development. You could not apply for a resettlement flat. You were offered one if your hut was about to be pulled down" (*Hong Kong Annual Review* 1991, p. 9).

Both Drakakis-Smith (1973) and Kehl (1981) identify the shortage of land and the consequent need to clear the squatter areas to make land available for development as the main reason for introducing the housing resettlement programme. They recognize that the land was to be used not only to house the immigrant population but also to develop industry. They go further to allege that the government intervened in order to maximize the production of land for the private sector to support the property development industry. According to them, since a large amount of government revenues were derived from land, it was natural for the government to be concerned about squatter encroachment on land that was worth developing. As we shall see later, their thesis of government intervention to support the property development industry has no merit.

The Political Argument

The clearance of squatter areas and the development of resettlement estates have often been associated with a public concern for social stability and social control. This political interpretation of the resettlement programme was developed by Smart (1992) in an important contribution on squatter clearance. Smart points out that the economic argument to make land available for development only explains the need for squatter clearance; it fails to "explain why the cleared squatters should be provided with public housing, a programme very much at odds with Hong Kong's traditions and the preferences of its government and its influential businessmen".

Smart goes on to argue that "the potential for resistance by squatters, resistance which could potentially result in political instability, is the missing factor in the equation. Squatter clearance without re-housing could be difficult and was potentially a source of danger to the government functionaries carrying out the clearance, and of disruption in a political system which was diplomatically threatened by the rise to power of the Chinese Communist Party".

An analogous concern was to emerge later in the wake of the social disturbances in the late 1960s. According to Castells, Goh, and Kwok (1990), Governor Murray MacLehose decided to use the public housing programme as the harbinger of his social reform policy. His objective was to minimize social dissension, rebuild the community, improve the channels of communication between the government and the grass roots, and encourage some limited forms of political participation to improve the effectiveness of government administration.

The Political Economy Argument

An alternative political economy argument was given a central role
in the study conducted by Lui (1984) in his interpretation of the role
of the state in subsidizing the industrialization of Hong Kong.
Cheap public housing was, according to their analyses, the key
instrument for reproducing labour power at a reasonable cost to
support industrialization.

The explanation was an attempt to demonstrate that the
capitalist state was an instrument for perpetuating and supporting
the capitalist mode of production. Subsidized public housing was a
device used to provide minimal housing support so that capitalists
could continue exploiting workers without risking the collapse of
capitalism. Implicit in their argument is also a criticism of the
laissez-faire model of economic development and its relevance for
explaining the economic success of Hong Kong.

Nowadays a somewhat modified version of the story is being
told, as intellectual hostility towards capitalism has receded somewhat with the demise of communist and socialist ideologies.
Today's story emphasizes the positive role of the state in supporting
capitalist development rather than its negative role in trying to avert
a capitalist collapse. Public support for the public housing programme is seen as one of the main instruments of the state by which
to promote development and economic hyper-growth. The main
theme of this account is that capitalism left to its own mechanisms is
still filled with internal economic contradictions.

It has been asserted that the rapid rates of economic growth
experienced in East Asia are not the result of the operation of free
markets and limited governments, as has been claimed by
neo-classical economists, but are rather the result of the guiding
hand of a benign developmental state. This claim is most forcefully
asserted by Castells, Goh, and Kwok (1990), who ultimately
identify Hong Kong's housing programme and economic success
with the reformist zeal of governor Murray MacLehose. Campo
and Root (1996) rely on the work of Castells, Goh and Kwok
(1990) and draw the conclusion that the public housing programme

was a mechanism by which to share wealth. The public housing programme therefore preserved social stability in a process of rapid economic growth and contributed to long-term economic development.

Inadequacies of Previous Analyses

The Political Economy Argument

There are two fatal flaws in the political economy argument. First, the direct provision of cheap government housing need not lower wages, as is alleged in the study conducted by Lui (1984). In a competitive labour market in which industries are export oriented, wages have to be determined by the productivity of workers in Hong Kong and the level of wages in the world market. There is no reason to believe that firms could benefit from housing subsidies unless they were able to offer lower wages to workers who occupy public housing units. This could not happen in a competitive market. Moreover, there is no evidence that firms paid discriminating wages.

A more subtle form of wage discrimination is the practice of labour market segregation. Firms may attempt to lower wage payments by hiring only those workers who live in public housing in the belief that their wage demands will be lower because of the housing subsidies. There is, however, no evidence that industrial firms hired predominantly workers who lived in public housing estates. The 1961, 1971, and 1981 censuses of population show that the occupational characteristics of tenants who lived in public housing units were not very different from those of tenants who lived in private housing units. It appears that discrimination based on labour market segregation did not exist.

The fact that the housing subsidy was provided to all workers and not just to industrial workers clearly shows the fallacy of the political economy argument. Furthermore, the subsidy was made through the direct provision of public housing. The number of units that were constructed each year limited the beneficiaries of the programme. As a consequence, a small fraction of the population will benefit each year. Even if the policy worked it would appear to be a very clumsy way of providing support for industrialization. A rental subsidy would be far more effective. The failure of the analysts who put forth the political economy argument to see the difference between a rental subsidy and a housing subsidy in the form of direct provision of housing units probably explains the flaw in their analysis.

Secondly, one must recognize the fact that government public housing subsidies provided to industrial workers to support industrialization are not free. They have an opportunity cost that must be borne by other workers who do not receive these subsidies but have to pay for them either explicitly or implicitly. There is also no reason to believe that society is better off because it supports the industrial sector at the expense of other sectors, unless one assumes at the outset that the economy is suffering from a peculiar form of market failure that can only be remedied through a government housing subsidy. Any economist would find such an argument very bizarre because there are other more efficient ways to support industrialization directly.

Perhaps the authors who crafted the political economy argument may be excused for making such a fundamental mistake because they are not trained in economic analysis. It is embarrassing to note, however, that even the World Bank's Policy Research Report *The East Asian Miracle* (1993) makes the same error. The report states that "the wide availability of low-cost housing for workers [in Hong Kong] helped to hold down wage demands, subsidizing labour-intensive manufacturing" (p. 163). This is indeed a grave error and reveals the infectious influence of such misguided thinking.

The Political Argument

The clearance of squatter areas and the development of the resettlement estates in the 1950s and 1960s have often been associated with a public concern for social stability and social control. Smart (1992) conjectures that political considerations — fear of civil disturbance and the rising diplomatic power of Communist China — might have been on the minds of the decision makers. Social stability and social control considerations taken alone are unlikely to be convincing explanations for the origins of the public housing programme. Indeed, a survey conducted in 1957 by the University of Hong Kong revealed two surprising findings. First, housing conditions in the resettlement estates were no worse than those in most of the slum tenements and, second, the living conditions in the squatter areas were found to be better than those in the slum tenements (Bray 1952, Maunder and Szczepanik 1957, Maunder 1969).

One would assume that, based on these findings, the most natural clients of the public housing programme would be tenants living in private slum tenements rather than those living in squatter settlements. Are we to believe that tenants who live in cramped slum tenements are less likely to pose a threat to social stability and that they present less of a problem for social control than squatters do who live on the fringes of urban areas in more spacious conditions? The fact that the resettlement estates were built to minimum standards makes the political argument even more unconvincing. Is the concern over public order and safety largely a figment of the imagination or a convenient excuse?

Furthermore, Johnson (1966) found that according to the 1961 population census there was no significant difference between the arrival dates of squatters and of non-squatters to Hong Kong. Evidence from surveys conducted by the University of Hong Kong in 1952 and 1957 show that emigrants from the city centre and fresh immigrants from China were equally likely to be squatters. These findings suggest that there must have been significant movement of households between squatting and permanent housing and that there is no obvious difference between the two groups except their preference for different types of accommodation. Hopkins (1971) notes that "contrary to first impressions, life in squatter settlements has solid advantages over life in many overcrowded private tenements". He finds that "squatters should not be seen in simple terms as poor; they do not constitute the poorest sector of the community".

An analogous concern emerged in the 1970s and 1980s in the wake of the social disturbances in the late 1960s. Castells, Goh, and Kwok (1990) emphasize Governor Murray MacLehose's reforming zeal and desire to pacify social dissension. But this explains the growth and development of the public housing programme after its establishment, not its origins. It is well known that once started, public programmes tend to have a life of their own and can grow in a way that bears little resemblance to what was originally intended.

The Economic Argument

The argument that the resettlement programme was introduced in order to clear the land occupied by squatters for development is correct but incomplete. As the post-war economy grew, the demand for land became acute. There were two possible ways to address this demand. The first was to redevelop the old built-up areas, and the second was to clear the squatter areas.

After the squatter settlements were cleared, the immediate problem of what would happen to the squatters and where they would go presented itself. The government officials responsible for clearing the squatter settlements had to address this question. A government programme to build resettlement housing appeared to them to be the only feasible and practical solution. In the absence of a government resettlement programme, the squatters would only settle in new areas. What this implied was that squatter clearance would become an unending activity as displaced squatters sought out new settlement areas.

If political considerations figured into the government's decision, it might have been the fear of having to disrupt the lives of many squatters over and over again that provided the impetus for the resettlement programme. Squatter clearance would have had to go on indefinitely unless a permanent housing solution could be found for displaced squatters. One must appreciate the fact that officials and other observers at the time were convinced that the private sector was not capable of responding to the massive housing needs that it was presented with. It is doubtful that any government official would have been willing to risk the unpopularity he or she would have incurred by being the instigator of repeated squatter clearance actions.

The Neglected Effects of Rent Control

In most discussions of the public housing programme, no reference is made to the parallel interventions pursued by the government in the private housing market. From an economic perspective, the private and public housing sectors are clearly linked on both the supply and demand sides. Any analysis that omits such a link would have to be considered seriously if not fatally flawed. The imposition of rent controls on pre-war private housing, although never regarded as a major cause of the rise of the public housing programme, is, according to our subsequent analysis, the single most important factor that crippled the private sector response in housing development. Rent control made it impossible for private developers to redevelop the existing housing stock for a long time. Their only possible response was to develop illegal squatter housing.

When redevelopment was finally facilitated later on, it led to a rush of redevelopment that in turn led to massive displacements and worsened the squatter situation. The government was compelled to escalate its housing programme. There is little doubt that rent control was directly responsible for setting the stage for government provision of housing.

The large public housing programme has also been an important factor in driving private developers out of the low-end housing market. Scarce land resources were therefore inefficiently utilized and as the public sector grew. As the economy became more affluent, the increasing inefficiency of the housing sector contributed to rising property prices and housing rentals in the private market. Perversely, this has made it politically impossible for the government to refrain from intervening in the housing market to provide ever more generous subsidies to tenants who aspire to live in and own better housing than they can afford.

The Proper Question to Answer

Although the public housing programme continues to be regarded by most observers as a major achievement in the post-war history of the territory, it is now generally perceived as being in need of major reform. First, the public housing sector is clearly too large to be managed efficiently. Second, left to its own mechanisms, the programme threatens to grow ever bigger as the public housing constituency continues to gain political strength and attempts to entrench its already considerable interests even further. Third, there is a growing recognition that the diverse housing needs of an increasingly affluent population are poorly served by a planning approach delivered by a government bureaucracy. The housing demands of the elderly, of small households, and for home ownership are too diverse to be met this way. Fourth, the large housing subsidies provided to well-off tenants in the public sector who refuse to leave has been a source of constant embarrassment for the government, especially when many less well-off tenants either have to live in squalid temporary housing or to pay high rents for private premises.

One does not have to investigate these problems in any great detail or to be equipped with a formidable analytical apparatus to appreciate the difficulties that plague the public housing programme. Even a casual reading of the consultative document, *A Review of Public Housing Allocation Policies*, issued by the Housing Authority in April 1984 will suffice to demonstrate the many contradictions of the public housing programme. The document contains a candid and useful review of policy issues in five problem areas and proposes an array of solutions. Unfortunately, as we shall discuss in great detail later, the solutions themselves have contradictory implications that would only lead to further complications.

The public housing programme in Hong Kong developed over a period of almost half a century. It included many different programmes that were the result of a number of different policies. The objectives behind these policies were not always consistent with each other. Some policies were in part a reaction to unfolding events and others were designed to address contemporaneous concerns that have since changed. Also, as the programme grew in size and complexity, various entrenched interests within the public housing constituency, which has come to dominate the housing policy agenda, have increasingly held the programme hostage.

Housing issues must be examined as part of a larger set of questions. It is not sufficient to discuss the merits and flaws of specific policy objectives. The achievements and failures of the policy cannot be assessed and evaluated against a set of criteria that are confined to specific housing goals, such as the number and quality of units built, the number and types of people accommodated, and the cost effectiveness of the programme.

The limitations of such a narrowly focused approach are obvious. It fails to provide a broad framework for understanding the rationale and objectives of government housing policy decisions in the first place. It also fails to delineate and anticipate the way in which the effects and outcomes of housing policies interact with society as a whole. Housing policy decisions are therefore taken as isolated datum rather than as the outcomes of social, economic, and political processes. Policy outcomes are analysed and evaluated in a static manner and without regard for their dynamic effects on other societal processes and outcomes. Such an approach also reinforces the tendency of established interests within the public housing constituency to dominate the housing policy agenda.

As government housing policies change over time, such an approach to policy analysis is crippling. The discontinuities and inconsistencies of government housing policies are therefore mirrored in the public discussions themselves. In failing to rise above or go beyond narrow housing issues, these discussions ultimately fail to provide us with any deep understanding of the housing problem. They cannot help us to avoid time-inconsistent policies that are inevitably very costly for society to correct in the future.

Time inconsistency is a term used by economists to describe a situation that occurs over time in which policy objectives are inconsistent with policy outcomes. This happens when the responses to policy actions lead to unintended consequences that are the opposite of the initial policy objectives. The failure to anticipate the consequences stems from the failure to recognize the fact that housing behaviour is part of a larger societal process that cannot be treated and analysed in isolation. These unintended consequences have an effect on future policy decisions and behaviour. The process is therefore considered to be path dependent in the sense that earlier decisions lead to outcomes that constrain the choices available and limit the actions that can be taken at a later stage. With path-dependent processes and time-inconsistent policies, the typical, narrowly-focused housing policy discussion is of limited value in helping us to understand and resolve our current housing predicament.

An adequate explanation of the rise and subsequent development of the public housing programme must first show why it was necessary for the government to subsidize housing development. If the private sector failed to adequately meet the housing needs of the massive influx of immigrants, then the reasons for this failure have to be accounted for. Second, the explanation must also provide an account of why public subsidy took the form of direct provision rather than a rental subsidy financed by the sale of cleared land, which the government could easily have implemented and is likely to have preferred (given its inclination for market-oriented solutions) at least in the period before Murray MacLehose became governor.

Public housing policies have important economic, social, and political effects that go far beyond the narrow confines of housing and accommodation concerns alone. By virtue of its enormous scale, the public housing programme will have implications for economic efficiency and social equity that cannot be ignored in any policy discussion. It is natural and fitting that housing policies should be addressed in a broader framework that also includes an evaluation of their many effects.

In order to deal properly with these questions — namely, *why* has there been a public housing programme in Hong Kong and *what* has its actual contribution been to the economic development and social well-being of the territory — it is first necessary to provide a fresh account of the precise profile of the public housing programme and related developments. It is also necessary to reinterpret that history so that we can arrive at a new understanding of the public housing problem. It is my contention that after forty years the public housing programme has arrived at a point where its internal contradictions and the problems it has created for society can only be reversed and remedied if we embark on a process of complete privatization of the public housing stock. The social and economic consequences of failing to do so will be colossal.

This study will examine why privatizing the public housing stock is the only practical and desirable solution to the housing situation. I believe there is a strong case for the position that housing policy should not be defined by housing concerns alone. This is the fatal flaw of many public housing reform proposals. Any sensible policy proposal must have as its main concern the advancement of the interests of society as a whole. It should not be too narrowly focused and should not become hostage to the interests of the public housing constituency, which is at the end of the day a single-issue constituency that cannot truly represent the public interest. It is important to recognize, of course, that a practicable reform proposal has to be politically and economically feasible. Insofar as it is possible, these considerations have been taken into account in this study.

CHAPTER 2

Squatters, Rent Control, and the Origins of Public Housing

The origins of the public housing programme, according to most accounts, can be traced back to the disastrous fires that occurred in Shek Kip Mei in December 1953. Shortly afterwards the government embarked on a programme to clear squatter areas and resettle the homeless inhabitants. From this modest beginning, the housing resettlement programme grew into the largest government undertaking in an otherwise free-enterprise economy.

It is widely believed that the sudden massive influx of new immigrants from the mainland into Hong Kong was the single most important catalyst for the implementation of the public housing programme. Between 1945 and 1951 massive immigration from China increased the local population from 600,000 to 2,360,000 (see Table 2.1). The demand for housing escalated suddenly. New immigrants invaded the fringes of urban areas. Squatter settlements mushroomed overnight.

Unfortunately, the process of urban redevelopment was severely complicated by impediments to private development and particularly by the imposition of rent control on pre-war housing. The situation became critical as the economy grew rapidly and the demand for housing increased. There was growing pressure on the government to either resettle squatters in order to clear the illegally occupied squatter settlements, or relax the conditions for evicting tenants for urban redevelopment purposes. Eventually the government did both. But we are jumping ahead of the story; let us start at the beginning. My discussion of the impediments to private

19

Table 2.1
Evolution of the Hong Kong Population

Year	Number of People
1901	386,229
1911	456,739
1921	625,166
1931	840,473
1941	1,639,337
1945	600,000
1947	1,800,000
1951	2,360,000
1961	3,129,648
1966	3,708,920
1971	3,900,000
1976	4,402,990
1981	4,986,560
1986	5,396,000
1991	5,522,281
1996	6,217,556
1997	6,617,100

Source: Chan (1986); Hambro (1995); Department of Census and Statistics, Hong Kong, *Hong Kong Annual Digest of Statistics 1996*; and *By-census Summary Report* 1996.

development and rent control and its consequences draws on the work by Smart (1992) and Cheung (1979). Smart's work is on the topic of squatter resettlement and Cheung's work is on the topic of rent control. These are separate and independent studies on two different subjects, and the two are brought together here for the first time in our analysis.

Understanding Squatter Settlements

Squatter clearance has always been regarded as the primary reason behind the implementation of the public housing programme. Unfortunately, inadequate knowledge of the process and history of squatter clearance has resulted in gross misinterpretation of the nature, causes, and effects of the public housing programme. It is important to be aware of the debate on the subject of the housing problem that took place in the Legislative Council in 1947 (*Hong Kong Hansard, 3 July 1947*, pp. 191–206).

In 1947 most of the Unofficial members of the Legislative Council were very critical of government impediments to private development and building and called on the government to remove all unnecessary regulatory barriers. The Unofficial members were representatives of property and business interests. In the 1947 Legco debate there were demands for the lowering of crown rents and premiums, the relaxation of the high degree of control exercised through lease conditions over what developers built, and the speeding up of lease transferrals within the administration. Councillors who were not governments officials, the "Unofficials", argued for a reduction in the number of obstacles standing in the way of private development. These voices were effectively brushed aside because Officials made up the majority in the Legislative Council. It is worth noting that all the Unofficials voted against the government.

This issue was important politically because through the Crown monopoly of land ownership, the imposition of numerous lease conditions and the use of the Building Ordinance to vet all development proposals meant that no new development or redevelopment could occur without extensive consultation with the government. Because of this, development could not take place quickly or easily. When housing was in high demand, the ensuing bottlenecks resulted in high land prices at auction and in expensive housing prices and rents.

The Unofficial members of the Legislative Council realized that the situation had to be remedied before private development could begin to occur quickly and profitably. Unfortunately, according to Smart (1992), "for a combination of technical reasons, bureaucratic interests, distrust of private developers as speculators, concern for government revenues, a commitment to town planning and building standards, and a concern on the part of some officials that the workers not be exploited by high rents and low standards, the government resisted these pressures" (pp. 38–39).

Between 1945 and 1948 the total number of persons in Hong Kong had already increased from 600,000 to 1,800,000. Nevertheless, in 1948 there were only 30,000 squatters in the territory, which represented only 2% of the population. This shows that the private sector had managed to house essentially the entire population within the existing housing stock, albeit in highly cramped conditions. Even by 1953, when there were 300,000 squatters, they made up only 10% of the total population. From these figures one would conclude that the most pressing housing problem in Hong Kong during the immediate post-war years was not squatter settlements but congestion in private tenements. The problem had to be solved through new developments and through redevelopment of the existing housing stock.

From 1945 to 1958 no more than 200 acres of land were made available in the urban area, and less than 30 acres were auctioned. The rest of the land on which building took place was granted by private treaty, primarily for non-profit projects. Clearly, an important factor affecting the housing shortage was the amount of new land made available for housing. There were only two private sector alternatives to creating living space for the population. One of these was redevelopment, but impediments stemming from rent control made this difficult. The second alternative was to increase the size and number of squatter settlements.

Given all these constraints, the private sector accommodated the rapidly expanding population incredibly well, although the population paid for the cost in terms of high rents, overcrowding, and inadequate facilities. The private sector also produced a large amount of illegal housing in the form of squatter dwellings for rent and for purchase. While it is unclear what proportion of the squatter dwellings were self-constructed and what proportion were constructed for sale or rental, according to Smart (1992), based on contemporary documents, the sale and rental of squatter dwellings was very common. He cites a *South China Morning Post* editorial that urged "the government to form more sites for sale to builders to resolve the housing shortage since many squatters can afford regular dwellings" (31 December 1958).

Smart (1992) also claims that "many of the same or similar construction companies were building houses in squatter areas as in the legal private sector; certainly this must be the case for the more elaborate, multi-storey, reinforced concrete buildings" (p. 41). One of the official justifications for launching the housing resettlement programme was that "by this resettlement programme we are breaking a 'racket'. . . . [I]n fact the squatter who owns his own hut is rare; most squatters are paying an exorbitant rent for the hut or more usually for the part of a hut which they occupy. . . . If we can give these people living space at a fair rent, and if we can do this on a really large scale, we shall knock the bottom out of a 'racket' which helps to keep the cost of living up" (*Hong Kong Hansard*, 2 March 1955, p. 40). What is particularly interesting in this quoted passage is the official position, which I should add is a mistaken one, that associates high rents and prices with the building of squatter units. Clearly rents and prices would be even higher if such activities did not take place.

It is worth noting that very often there were only two real distinctions between squatter settlements that were illegal and the rest of the private housing sector.[1] First, the former were built on agricultural land that had not been converted to building land and, second, the construction had not been subjected to government vetting in accordance with the Building Ordinance. Squatter settlements on agricultural land are particularly interesting in that the squatters often paid rent to the landowner. The landowners themselves often sold or rented out the land to relatives and sometimes even to strangers. The illegal structures can therefore be viewed as a private sector initiative that overcame the barriers to development imposed by the government. They succeeded by going beyond the bounds of legality.

The government intervention in the market had effectively choked off the private sector's response to the post-war housing situation except through the construction of illegal squatter housing. In an important sense, it was not the private sector that had failed to meet the rising demand for housing following the massive influx of immigrants that forced the government to step in; rather, the government was primarily responsible for worsening the housing situation and creating the squatter settlements. By insisting on preserving its extensive control over the development process, the government effectively crippled any possible private sector development. In failing to respond to the dramatically different housing situation in the post-war period, the government set in motion forces that would eventually compel it to assume direct responsibility for housing the bulk of Hong Kong's population.

Development of Rent Control Legislation, 1947–55

In October 1945, at the end of the Second World War, the British Military Administration made an emergency proclamation to clamp down on rents on all existing pre-war premises following the retrocession of Hong Kong by the Japanese forces. The proclamation was intended to protect the masses of returning Hong Kong residents against inflationary rentals. Discrimination against non-residents and new immigrants was implicit. In May 1947 the Landlord and Tenancy Ordinance was enacted to control rent on all pre-war premises, both domestic and business. The rents charged on pre-war premises were set with reference to their pre-war levels.

The 1947 ordinance protected the interest of tenants occupying pre-war premises by limiting the increases in rent to 30% of the standard rent that landlords could charge for domestic premises. The standard rent was defined as the rent payable for the unfurnished premises on or most recently before 25 December 1941. The Tenancy Tribunal was created to make judicial decisions regarding landlord-tenant matters and to determine the amount of rent payable with respect to pre-war premises.

Several rent increases have been authorized since 1947, but increases in rents have lagged behind market rents. An increase of 55% of standard rent for domestic premises was allowed in 1954. This 55% increase remained frozen for over twenty years until December 1975, when the permitted increase on standard rent was raised to 105% for domestic premises. Meanwhile, rent in the uncontrolled sector had skyrocketed.

The original rent control enactment was intended to last for only a year, but after extensions were granted each year, the termination provision was finally deleted in 1953. From then on the Landlord and Tenant Ordinance constituted an effective body of laws. Only recently did it start to be phased out.

Under the original 1947 ordinance a landlord could repossess a building for reconstruction, but the tenants would reserve the right to possession. There were only two ways for a landlord to repossess a building: eviction or exemption. Given that the ordinance was written to protect the interests of the tenant and was entirely biased against landlords, eviction was almost impossible in practical terms.[2]

When the gains from reconstruction were substantial, a landlord could bribe his tenants to quit the premises. Although monetary payments were made illegal under the 1947 ordinance, this was not a major obstacle. The more difficult issue to resolve was the problem of holdouts. It was hard to make progress in such negotiations because there would always be some tenants who would demand more than their fair share of the landlord's potential gain.[3]

Repossession by application to the Tenancy Tribunal for exemption from the 1947 ordinance was also problematic. The Tenancy Tribunal's decisions were based primarily on considerations of public interest, which was often interpreted to mean the social desirability of safeguarding the low rentals enjoyed by the occupying tenants. Redevelopment and reconstruction were not considered to be part of the public interest. As a consequence, many landlords were unwilling to bear the high cost of making applications and attending court hearings under such uncertain and adverse conditions.[4]

In actual practice, therefore, the cost of repossessing pre-war premises under rent control for redevelopment and reconstruction was made prohibitive by the legal process. It was almost impossible to repossess existing premises for reconstruction purposes. This severely limited the incentive for private developers to undertake housing reconstruction during the immediate post-war years. It is a mistake to conclude that this was a case of market failure. A market solution was rendered impossible from the very beginning because of rent control. An interventionist solution in the form of a public housing programme soon appeared as a practical solution.

Problems began to emerge as a result of the difficulties of repossessing buildings. By 1953 many buildings were faltering and uninhabitable. Landlords had no incentives to maintain or repair old buildings, since they could neither raise rents nor reconstruct buildings to realize any capital gains. As a result, many buildings became hazardous for tenants to occupy. An amendment in 1953 authorized the Director of Public Works to certify certain buildings as dangerous in order to allow for "vacant possession of the premises" by the landlord.[5] In such cases, tenants could be evicted without compensation. Landlords welcomed the decision, but tenants bitterly opposed it. Hostility between landlords and tenants increased.

The profits that could be made from reconstruction were enormous. Market rents soared in the uncontrolled post-war buildings due to surging demographic pressure and improving economic conditions. The "dangerous building" provision was attractive to landlords because tenants could be evicted without compensation if the case were approved on those grounds. It was rumoured that while performing repair works some landlords removed vital structures to make the building dangerous for inhabitation.

The Landlord and Tenant Ordinance was finally amended in 1955 to make it easier for a landlord to apply for exemption for reconstruction purposes. The Tenancy Tribunal was granted the power of eminent domain in these cases. Landlords would henceforth make a monetary compensation to the tenants for the loss of their tenancies.[6] This greatly reduced the transaction costs for evicting tenants as well as the tension between the two parties.

Changes in the Plot Ratio, 1955–61

Another change occurred after 1955 to make the gains from repossession even more attractive. The Building Ordinance (1935) was amended in 1956 to allow for the building of structures that were considerably taller than had previously been permitted.[7] The gains from evicting tenants thus rose dramatically. The pressure to reduce the cost of repossessing buildings for reconstruction purposes mounted.

These two amendments dramatically increased the number of successful exemption cases, as tenants became more receptive to negotiations with their landlords.[8] Together the amendments led to a belated surge in housing reconstruction, which reached a peak in 1959, when some 12,000 private domestic units were built. The surge in property redevelopment demonstrates the falsehood of the contention that the private sector was unable to respond to the housing crisis created by the massive population influx. The real issues were incentives and costs.

In addition to ruling on reconstruction proposals, the Tenancy Tribunal was also granted the power to determine the amount of compensation. It is obvious that the pace of urban renewal would have been reduced if the amount of compensation was set at a level that was too high, and *vice versa*. The compensation rate was in fact set too low. However, the problem of premature reconstruction was not serious in the late 1950s because rent control had delayed housing construction for over ten years. Many existing structures were overdue for demolition.

Within a narrow time span the demolition of numerous old buildings, which had been delayed for a decade, led to a short-run worsening of the housing situation. Large numbers of evicted tenants became squatters. Saturation of market demand thereafter caused a decline in building activity until after 1961.

Unfortunately, the Tenancy Tribunal decided to allow the rate structure of compensation to be essentially frozen throughout the period from the late 1950s to the early 1970s. Meanwhile, market rents skyrocketed in the 1950s and early 1960s. This provided landlords with a very large incentive to repossess buildings for reconstruction, since tenants could be evicted with relatively low monetary compensation. The stage was set for the rush towards excessive reconstruction. The disastrous building rush that took place in 1962–65 was due partly to the low compensation rate structure.

Further Changes in the Plot Ratio, 1962–65

The high intensity of reconstruction in the late 1950s increased urban congestion, led to uneven urban development, and imposed severe strains on the transportation system and on the provisioning of utility services. In a bid to reduce congestion the government then decided to scale down the permitted intensity of development by amending the Building Ordinance. However, an odd event soon took place and resulted in a frenzied outburst of reconstruction activity from 1962 to 1965.

On 19 September 1962 a plot ratio amendment to restrict the ratio of gross floor space to area of the site was enacted to take effect in October 1962. The result of this amendment was that landlords would end up with less floor space than was permitted in the amended 1955 Ordinance. Initially, the amendment was expected to delay housing construction, since it lowered the prospective rents of a new building.

Oddly enough, a loophole in an "Explanatory Note" attached to the amendment essentially provided an escape clause that allowed reconstruction plans submitted before the end of 1965 to be exempted from the new restrictions and to be approved under the original 1955 provisions. Since the new plot ratio implied a decrease in the supply of floor space in the future, it was in the interest of the landlord to beat the deadline.

Thus, during the grace period between 1962 and 1965, there was an unprecedented wave of private residential development. Plans were afoot to have one-third to one-half of the pre-war premises rebuilt in a period of three years (Cheung 1979, p. 47). The housing market would soon become vastly oversupplied. But before this occurred, construction delays and excessive demolition of older buildings would exacerbate the shortage in accommodations. As a consequence, rents in post-war premises escalated sharply. The first comprehensive rent control legislation, called the Rent Increases (Domestic Premises) Control Ordinance, was enacted in 1963 to control increases in rent of post-war domestic accommodation. The ordinance was allowed to expire in 1966 because of a market glut that occurred as a result of the excessive reconstruction activity in the interim years. Demolition of buildings also lead to mass evictions of existing tenants, and the squatter situation worsened. The squatter population peaked in 1964, coinciding with the peak number of evictions from tenements (Drakakis-Smith 1973, p. 25).

In 1965 a considerable falling off in the rate of development had already been felt. This downward trend was reflected in the fact that a total of 885 exemption orders were made in 1964, but the number dropped to 200 in 1965 and to only 25 in 1966. By 1966, 18,000 domestic units were vacant.

An economic depression soon set in. A minor run on the banks in 1964 was followed by a surge of heavier bank runs in 1965 that even affected the largest Chinese bank. It is widely believed that the reconstruction craze of 1963–65 precipitated a bank panic. The housing boom collapsed into a deep depression that lasted from mid-1965 until late 1969. Rental values dropped by 40%, and property values plunged an estimated 70% to 80%. Half-built structures were everywhere. Landlords would now routinely apply for extensions to postpone commencement or completion of building works. Pending applications for exemption were withdrawn. The riots of 1967 probably intensified the depression, although one could probably make a case for the converse as well. The harsh and uncertain economic condition of the time created a tense social situation in which even minor incidents easily flared up into crises. The human and economic costs were immeasurable.

Rent Control Legislation after 1968

In 1968 the Landlord and Tenant Ordinance was further amended to permit landlords to negotiate directly with their tenants for a surrender or termination of their tenancy in return for compensation.[9] Landlords were hence no longer obligated to use reconstruction as an excuse to raise rents to market levels. The amendment headed off some premature reconstruction after the economy started to recover in the early 1970s.

By the end of 1969 the economy began to pick up from the depression. Market rents started to rise because the existing rent control ordinance no longer applied to the majority of the units in the private market. Most of the pre-war units had been torn down during the reconstruction boom. Tenants who had been accustomed to stable rents protested. The government imposed again rent control on post-war housing as a temporary measure. The Rent Increases Control Ordinance was enacted in June 1970. The ordinance covered the majority of tenancies and sub-tenancies in post-war domestic premises completed or substantially rebuilt after 16 August 1945.

The regulations controlling pre-war and post-war premises were consolidated into legislation in the Landlord and Tenant (Consolidation) Ordinance of 1972. The 1947 ordinance was re-enacted as Part I of the consolidated ordinance and formed the basis for regulating pre-war premises. Controls regarding post-war premises were spelled out in Part II of the new ordinance.

The disastrous effects of rent control on property values and private housing development prompted the government to gradually decontrol rents seven years after the enactment of the consolidated ordinance. In 1979 legislation was passed to exclude controls on tenancies in pre-war buildings for business purposes to take effect on 1 July 1984, allowing a five-year adjustment period.

In 1980 an amendment permitting "self-use" as a legitimate ground for possession, which favoured landlords over sitting tenants, was made.[10] This amendment coincided with the property boom in the early 1980s, and landlords were delighted to obtain vacant possession of flats, even though the law required that the landlord who had repossessed the premise must live there for two years before selling or renting it out again.

A committee established to review the Landlord and Tenant (Consolidation) Ordinance issued a report in 1981 to speed up the process of decontrolling rents. The committee aimed to abolish rent controls in the private domestic sector but to maintain a degree of security of tenure by giving the tenants the right to renew tenancy at market rents.

With respect to pre-war premises, increases in rent have been permitted periodically. In May 1981 legislation was amended to provide for permitted rent for domestic premises to be eight times the standard rent, and in subsequent years the legislation was amended each year to raise the permitted rent. The most recent amendment took place in November 1990, when the permitted rent was allowed to be raised to forty-eight times the standard rent.

Other progressive decontrol measures were adopted for post-war premises. The Landlord and Tenant (Consolidation) (Amendment) Bill of 1992 proposed to eliminate rent controls by the year 1994, affecting some 39,000 private housing tenants. The proposed legislation was amended in July 1993 to delay the phasing out of rent control until the end of 1996. But a resolution passed in December 1996 further extended the period of phasing out to 31 December 1998. The resilience of rent control legislation is truly amazing.

It is indeed a great blessing for Hong Kong that the most onerous effects of rent control have been progressively eliminated through a series of amendments. It is clear that rent control has been primarily responsible for the high degree of volatility in the building cycles and in property prices in Hong Kong that have at times threatened the integrity of the banking system. It is a tribute to those within and without the government who, despite earlier mistakes, have finally managed to bring us back from the brink of disaster. Many years ago the Swedish economist Assar Lindbeck identified rent control as the best way of destroying a city, short of bombing it. The main lesson to be learned from Hong Kong's history is that rent control has been responsible to a large extent for the rise of squatter settlements and the public housing programme. Today rent control is fortunately no longer an important policy issue, but its effects continue to be felt in the large public housing stock Hong Kong has inherited.

An Assessment of the Consequences of Rent Control

The origin of the public housing programme was the massive inflow of immigrants in the 1940s. This created an enormous housing shortage and resulted in overcrowding in private tenements. The supply of new land was limited, and private development was made difficult by administrative delays and government regulations. To make matters worse, rent control, originally devised as a temporary measure to protect the interests of local residents, was introduced. The imposition of rent control severely impeded the market adjustment process and made reconstruction of existing buildings almost impossible in the period 1947–55. Squatter settlements became the only solution to the housing problem.

The outcome was clear. The housing situation worsened, and the squatter problem could not be resolved. The situation became critical as the economy grew rapidly and housing demand increased. There was growing pressure on the government to either resettle squatters in order to clear the illegally occupied squatter settlements, or relax the conditions for evicting tenants for urban redevelopment purposes. The government did both. In fact, the decision to resettle large numbers of squatters into multi-storeyed public resettlement blocks after the fire in December 1953 was made before and independent of the amendment to the Landlord and Tenancy Ordinance in August 1955.

When land occupied by squatters was needed for urban development, the government had to introduce a resettlement programme for the squatters. The public housing programme was extended to private renters, many of whom were evicted from private slum tenements in the wake of the reconstruction boom in the late 1950s and early 1960s. The development of the low-cost government housing programme in 1962 can also be attributed to the effects of rent control. From then on, the public housing programme was to experience exponential growth in the next three decades. By reacting to unfolding events, the government has committed itself to a large programme of public housing provision in Hong Kong.

By choosing to impose rent control in 1945, the government set in motion a sequence of events whose consequences have continued to plague Hong Kong's people. This account attempts to dispel some of the commonly held myths about the origins of the public housing policy. The history of rent control in Hong Kong illustrates how one form of market intervention creates the conditions that lead to further intervention.

It is only when the scale of intervention becomes so massive and its ill effects become so apparent that we come to recognize them as such. But by then so many vested interests have been created that the system becomes almost impossible to reform. To its credit, the government had the wisdom to remove rent controls, but the public housing programme will be much more difficult to eradicate. The Housing Authority has been considering privatization of the public housing stock and to re-creating the housing market that it has gradually taken over.

The surge of reconstruction in the late 1950s and the housing boom in 1962–65 rejects conclusively the often-heard assertion that the private sector was simply unable to cope with the task of housing the massive influx of immigrants in the post-war period. The responsiveness of private developers in the periods during which rent control was relaxed demonstrated that the market response could work very well.

The development of squatter settlements was itself a private initiative. There is considerable evidence that many squatter dwellings were constructed for sale or rental. Only the issue of illegality differentiates the building of squatter dwellings for commercial reasons from the rest of the private-sector housing development. These illegal structures are the products of private sector ingenuity, which overcame the impediments laid down by the government by going beyond the bounds of legality.

These final observations suggest that rather than the private sector being unable to cope with the demand for housing and the state eventually being forced, for whatever reason, to intervene, the state was chiefly responsible for preventing the private sector from functioning properly. Had it not been for the private sector, many immigrants would not even have a squatter dwelling to call home.

Notes

1. The idea that illegal structures represented the distorted development of market institutions due to heavy government regulations was pioneered by Hernando de Soto (1990) in his path-breaking work on the Peruvian informal sector. Smart (1992) probably applied a similar but rudimentary form of these ideas to the study of squatter housing in Hong Kong without knowing of the work by the former.

2. Cheung (1979) reports that he was unable to find even a single case of successful eviction.

3. Cheung (1979) failed to locate any record of successful agreements with all tenants for reconstruction.

4. Cheung (1979) found that fewer than 100 exemption orders leading to reconstruction were granted from 1947 to 1954.

5. Ordinances of Hong Kong 1953, No. 22, section 3A, cited in Cheung (1979).

6. The amendment was made following the ruling of the Tenancy Tribunal in the case of Mrs. Lee Pik-fu vs. Kwan Cheong (Cheung 1979, pp. 5–46).

7. 1956 Hong Kong Government Gazette, G.N. A45, Proclamation No. 1 cited in Cheung (1979).

8. Cheung (1979) reports that since 1955, about 75% of the pre-war housing reconstruction were approved through exemption. In the years before 1955, a total of fewer than 100 exemption cases were approved. In 1955 alone 104 cases were approved. In 1960 the number of approved exemption cases rose to 270.

9. Hong Kong Ordinances 1968, No. 40, A200 cited in Cheung (1979).

10. Ordinances of Hong Kong 1980, Landlord and Tenant (Consolidation) Ordinance 1980, No. 6.

CHAPTER 3

Growth of Public Housing from 1954 to 1983: An Alternative View

Hong Kong's public housing programme was put into effect in 1954. By 1983 some 45% of the population were living in public housing. The programme had become very large and expensive, and it was still growing. The government played a fairly passive role in providing public housing at the beginning. The massive influx of immigrants and the emergence of a huge squatter population had started to become major issues in 1945, but it was not until 1954 that the government began to provide public housing to resettle squatters. Until then, government intervention had been minimal.

The programme progressed through three different stages during the period 1954–83. In the first stage (1954–64), under the management of the Resettlement Department, its main objective was to resettle squatters to clear land for redevelopment. The target was to relocate 50,000 persons each year. The programme achieved this goal, and between 1954 and 1965 the resettlement estates housed a total of 607,673 persons.

In the second stage (1965–73), under the stewardship of the Housing Board, a ten-year building programme that would house on average 220,000 persons each year was announced. A number of different housing agencies were responsible for delivering several different types of housing units under a variety of schemes under the programme. At the end of the period the programme fell short of its initial target by more than 50%. An average of only 100,000 persons were housed each year.

In the third stage (1973–83), under the control of the Housing Authority, a new ten-year building programme was initiated with the aim of building enough units to house 1,535,000 persons. The programme was expected to satisfy the housing demands of different groups: squatters, tenants in resettlement estates to be redeveloped, and tenants in overcrowded public-sector housing estates. The programme also included an allowance for special factors and contingencies. It too fell short of its production target by 50%.

The fact that the public housing programmes fell short of their production targets in the last of the three stages is particularly surprising, because this stage represented the most ambitious housing building effort and was the centre-piece of the energetic governor Murray MacLehose's social reform policy. By contrast, the only public housing programme that met its targets was the relatively modest first-stage resettlement programme. A number of different factors contributed to the shortfall. These will be elaborated upon later in this chapter. It is useful to note at this point that the resettlement programme was relatively simple and straightforward to administer. The later-stage programmes were far more complex and involved constructing different types of housing and meeting the needs of different groups.

It appears that when the public housing programme was expected to deliver housing units beyond the bare minimum standard, administrative cost and other difficulties became so large that original targets could not be met. The disadvantage of the bureaucratic planning approach was most evident when it had to undertake complex tasks with multiple goals.

The Period 1954–64

In 1951 the government established "approved" areas in which squatters could build cottages made of fire-resistant materials and "tolerated" areas in which wooden huts could be erected. The government also partly financed two non-government housing agencies to help alleviate the housing pressure: the Hong Kong Housing Society was formed in 1951 to provide homes for lower middle-income families, and the Hong Kong Settlers' Housing Corporation was set up in 1952 to build cottages for occupants who would become owners after they had paid monthly rent for seven years.

The situation changed drastically after 1953. The squatter fire in Shek Kip Mei in December 1953 acted as the catalyst for direct government intervention in the provision of housing. The view that the public housing programme was introduced primarily to reclaim land for development is widely accepted. The Commissioner for Resettlement stated clearly that, "Squatters are not resettled simply because they need . . . or deserve, hygienic, and fireproof houses; they are resettled because the community can no longer afford to carry the fire risk, health risk, and threat to public order and prestige which the squatter areas represent and because the community needs the land on which they illegally occupy. And the land is needed quickly" (Commissioner for Resettlement, *Annual Report 1955*, p. 46).

In 1954 the Resettlement Department was formed with the object of squatter clearance and resettlement to make land available for urban development. The Department was put in charge of the task of building as quickly as possible and at the lowest possible cost housing estates that could allow for the relocation of squatters to more suitable sites. Resettlement estates were built by the Public Works Department and financed by public funds. The target was set at relocating 50,000 persons per year. In the first year 54,000 people were accommodated in eight newly constructed resettlement estates. By 1964–65 a total of 607,673 persons were accommodated in the completed resettlement estates (see Table 3.1).

In a parallel move, the government increased its support for the Housing Society and in 1954 established the Hong Kong Housing Authority to provide better public housing for people who were not squatters and who were in higher income brackets. Since priority

Table 3.1
Number of Persons Accommodated in Public Housing, 1955–65

Year	Cumulative Totals				Total
	Resettlement Estates	Low Cost Housing	Housing Authority	Housing Society	
1954 / 55	30,255			3,658	33,913
1955 / 56	91,672			8,820	100,492
1958 / 59	150,774		16,158	17,100	184,032
1960 / 61	258,246		38,488	30,030	326,764
1962 / 63	398,269		68,353	40,870	507,492
1964 / 65	607,673	49,655	127,571	63,710	848,609

Source: Castells, Goh and Kwok (1990).

funding was provided to the Resettlement Programme, the achievements of the Housing Society and the Housing Authority were more modest. By 1964–65 the total number of persons accommodated was 63,710 and 127,571, respectively.

The work of the Resettlement Department in resettling squatters, who were cleared from land required for development, and the Housing Authority and the Housing Society, which provided limited accommodation to low-income families, was by any account impressive. But the squatter situation in 1964 was even worse than it had been in 1954. The number of squatters had actually increased from 300,000 in 1953 to 600,000 in 1964. By 1964 squatters represented over 20% of the population. What had happened?

The growth in the number of squatters between 1954 and 1964 cannot be attributed to the arrival of new immigrants, because the flow slowed down after 1954. The cumulative stock of new immigrants that arrived in the decade following the year 1954 could not have been more than a fifth of the total number of squatters that were resettled in the same period. Two others factors were responsible for the increase in the squatter population, and both were related to government policy decisions.

First, the displacement of tenement dwellers by private redevelopment operators forcing demolition in the older areas of the city led to a worsening of the housing situation. After rent control legislation was amended to facilitate redevelopment in 1955, a belated surge of reconstruction of pre-war housing stock took place. The surge turned into a speculative housing reconstruction boom in 1963–65. As we explained previously, this boom was triggered by an amendment that downgraded the plot ratio permitted by the Building Ordinance. Landlords rushed to beat the deadline for submitting redevelopment plans in order to take advantage of the old and higher plot ratio. When the property bubble burst in 1966 there was a huge oversupply of private flats. In 1966, 18% of the private housing units built during the previous twelve months were estimated to be unoccupied. Even worse, many buildings were not even completed. The escalating squatter situation was one of the consequences of having imposed rent control on pre-war premises.

Second, a policy to resettle squatters so as to clear the land for redevelopment inevitably creates a set of perverse incentives. The policy encouraged private housing tenants to become squatters to wait their chance of being offered resettlement. The government soon found itself engaged in the endless task of resettling squatters. The more people it resettled, the more people chose to become squatters. Indeed, surveys of squatter settlements in 1957 indicated that about half of the residents had lived in private housing before becoming squatters. One of the reasons they had opted to live in squatter settlements was the crowded living conditions in the private sector. These people were not necessarily poor; many were opportunists who were betting on the chance of being resettled.

The Period 1965–73

The issue of displaced private tenement tenants became increasingly serious as the pace of delayed urban redevelopment began to accelerate. Social pressure mounted for the government to provide housing support for lower-income households living in private

Table 3.2
Ten-year Building Programme, 1964–74

Category of Agency and Type of Housing Unit	Target Number of Persons to be Housed	Actual Production	
		Persons	Number of Flats
Resettlement Estates (standard: 2.2 m² per person)	1,900,000	661,000	130,000
Government Low Cost Housing (standard: 3.25 m² per person)	290,000	200,000	68,000
Housing Authority	85,000	105,000	18,000
Housing Society (Not a government agency)		74,000	13,000
Total	2,275,000	1,040,000	229,000
Annual average	220,000	100,000	23,000

Source: Castells, Goh and Kwok (1990), p. 23.

tenements. In 1961 the government introduced a Government Low Cost Housing Scheme to provide accommodation upon application for households living in overcrowded and sub-standard conditions with monthly incomes below HK$500. The Housing Authority was responsible for the management of all properties built under this scheme.

In 1964 a White Paper entitled *Review of Policies for Squatter Control, Resettlement and Government Low Cost Housing* was issued. It set out a comprehensive and ambitious ten-year housing plan. Production targets were set for 1.9 million resettlement units and 290,000 government low-cost housing units. The Housing Board was established in 1965 as an advisory board to the government to co-ordinate all the public housing programmes.

Nevertheless, the initiative fell short of its target by a considerable margin (see Table 3.2). The Government Low Cost Housing Scheme was slowed down because favourable loans and subsidies were halted as a result of the 1968 government decision that required the Housing Authority and Housing Society to become self-financing. This decision should not have affected the resettlement programme. The programme was probably delayed by a combination of factors. The housing depression in the private sector that followed the banking crisis of 1965, the uncertainty following the 1966 and 1967 riots, and the inefficiencies of coordinating a joint effort across a number of different government units in all likelihood each exacted a toll.

Did the massive subsidized public housing programme that provided benefits for a subset of the population have a positive effect on income distribution? Interestingly this question was not a policy concern at the beginning. The resettlement programme was designed to clear land for redevelopment and was not based on any concern about income redistribution effects. No attempt was made to institute a means test to identify the income levels of squatters to be relocated into resettlement estates. It became an issue only later with the introduction of the Government Low Cost Housing scheme, which was aimed at helping the poor. The appearance of two different objectives — squatter clearance and housing for the poor — created a major inconsistency within the public housing programme, although it was not recognized at the time. In the beginning, these different objectives were not necessarily in serious conflict with one another. Many squatters were among the most impoverished in society; therefore, by default, the resettlement programme probably ended up achieving the same result as the Government Low Cost Housing scheme.

For society this was a highly desirable social outcome. Akerlof (1978) shows that it was cheaper for society to redistribute income to a "tagged" group than to adopt a negative income tax scheme. A tagged group has an identifiable characteristic that is strongly correlated with conditions of poverty. The tagged group in this context are the squatters. As a consequence, redistributing income to this group would lead to a significant improvement in equality. Since membership in the tagged group was limited, it would ensure that marginal persons who were not truly impoverished would get

Table 3.3

Percentage of Public and Private Renter Households by Income Brackets, 1976

Household Income ($)	Public Renters (%)	Private Renters (%)
0– 399	8.25	9.67
400– 699	9.03	11.03
700– 899	10.31	10.75
900–1,099	11.37	10.19
1,100–1,299	11.81	10.26
1,300–1,564	11.54	10.01
1,565–1,899	12.25	9.39
1,900–2,399	11.47	9.26
2,400–3,399	10.00	9.21
3,400–	3.98	10.23
All Income Groups	100	100
No. of Households	34,058	32,054

Source: Based on data from 1976 By-Census of Population.

no benefits. The advantage of this feature is not present in a scheme like the negative income tax, which makes some transfers to all individuals.

Unfortunately, such a policy also encourages people to change or disguise their true characteristics in order to join the tagged group. This is precisely what happened when private housing tenants turned themselves into squatters. Once this phenomenon occurs, the policy of redistributing income to tagged groups is no longer as effective.

Even though means tests were introduced for those who applied under the Government Low Cost Housing scheme, they were not always an effective mechanism when applied in practice. The income eligibility criterion used was current family income at the time of admission to the programme. Households were not required to subject themselves to subsequent means tests in order to stay in the programme. Although this omission avoided certain disincentive effects on work effort, it also made it easier for families to misrepresent their true income, and it failed to take into account the future income prospects of the family.

Whom did the programme benefit? Surprisingly, until very recently there have been no easily accessible public data on the social profiles of the beneficiaries. Using data from public access files of the population By-Census in 1976, we are able to compare the income distribution of renters in the public housing sector with that of those in the private sector. Figures from Table 3.3 show that the distribution of income between the two sectors are not significantly different. It appears that despite a massive effort by the government to provide public housing for the poor and for squatters in the period 1964–74, there was no observable impact on income redistribution. The perception that those persons who lived in public housing were largely poor is a myth. Unfortunately, it was not recognized as such until quite recently.

The injustice of the situation might not have been appreciated by policy makers and other social commentators. It is astonishing that after thirty years during which public housing was available, there was little public data on the social and economic profiles of the public housing beneficiaries. Nevertheless households at the grassroots level could hardly be unaware through their immediate experiences of numerous incidences of injustice in the allocation of public housing resources.

The figures also show that at very low levels of income there were proportionately more private renters than public renters. This reflects in part the eligibility criteria that discriminated against small households. It explains why the waiting list for getting into public housing was so long. As long as there is a long waiting list, the demand for public housing will remain strong because of unmet demand from poor private renters.

The MacLehose Era: 1973–83

Murray MacLehose inherited a delicate social and political situation when he became governor. He identified social reform as one of the critical elements for accomplishing his key political assignment to pacify and stabilize the colony after the 1966 and 1967 riots. He realized that the grievances of an immigrant society had to be properly addressed. He devoted 80% of his first speech to the Legislative Council in October 1972 to social policy, with particular emphasis on housing. He stated that: "It is my conclusion that the inadequacy and scarcity of housing and all that this implies, and the harsh situation that results from it, is one of the major and most constant sources of friction and unhappiness between the government and the population. It offends alike our humanity, our civic pride and our political good sense" (pp. 2–3).

The perverse effects of a public housing programme resulted in a situation that appeared to many to be the *ad hoc* provision of large subsidies to one group in society at the expense of another group that was at least as, if not more, deprived. The injustice of the housing situation might not have been in the public conscience at that time, but the problem of poor housing conditions was recognized by all.

To his credit, MacLehose realized that the housing policy was the key element of a broader social policy to improve the well-being of the local population in a significant way. To this end, he called for a new housing policy to provide better-quality housing and programmes for a better integration of the population into pre-planned communities. He endorsed the concept of new towns that first emerged in the 1960s. In such towns, public housing, private housing, industrial units, and commercial facilities would intermix in a relatively self-contained area.

Tsuen Wan, where textile mills had already located in the 1950s, was the first of these new towns. Several public housing estates were built there in the late 1960s. MacLehose's plan was to develop several new towns in the New Territories. The first generation of new towns included Kwai Chung, Tsing Yi, Shatin, and Tuen Mun; the second generation included Yuen Long, Tai Po, and Fanling-Sheung Shui; and the third generation included Tseung Kwun O and Tin Shui Wai.

MacLehose's ambitious housing programme called for the construction of a total of 350,000 flats during the ten-year period.

An expected 1,535,000 people were to be accommodated. To manage the programme, all the existing housing agencies were unified in 1973 into a single institution, the Housing Authority. In quantitative terms, the number of units that were actually built by the Housing Authority fell far short of the target. A total of 176,623 rental units — only 50.4% of the target number — were constructed during the period. Part of the shortfall can be explained by the construction of 23,020 Home Ownership Scheme flats. The main failure, however, had to be the unrealistically ambitious plan. We have previously noted that bureaucratic agencies are poorly suited to implementing complex plans with multiple and changing objectives.

In pushing his housing plans, MacLehose met with considerable opposition even within his own civil service, especially from Sir Philip Haddon-Cave, the Financial Secretary. A number of observers have interpreted MacLehose's personal intervention in the policy-making and implementation process to ensure that his plan prevailed as illustrative of the importance of personality factors in a political system in which the governor essentially held absolute power.

Whatever the merits of this interpretation, it is useful to recall that the housing situation MacLehose inherited left him with very few options. He could not confidently rely on the private sector to perform the task at hand. Until then, private developers had been involved mainly in urban redevelopment and were often associated with worsening the squatter situation by evicting tenants from tenement units. The effectiveness and capability of private developers were believed to have been crippled by the most severe property market crash in Hong Kong's history. The economy had yet to recover from the self-inflicted depression, and there was still a general atmosphere of political uncertainty.

To move quickly to stabilize what was perceived as a tense social situation, Maclehose thought he had to rely on public programmes, which of course suited the social inclinations of the governor. Furthermore, by the time he arrived on the scene, the government was already heavily involved in resettling squatters.

The machinery was there; it appeared to be simply a matter of retooling it and giving it a new push and direction.

Public Housing Development — An Evaluation

The public housing programme had two major consequences: one economic the other political. Both have continued to exert a powerful influence on societal development today.

The Political Effects

The political effects of the housing programme had their origins in several important steps MacLehose took toward political reform. In 1972 city district committees and area committees were organized as consultative bodies to the district officers. The latter were first introduced in 1968 to improve communication between the administration and civil society. In 1973 the community-based structure expanded its reach with the development of mutual aid committees at the block level. The number of mutual aid committees grew from 1214 in 1973 to 3132 in 1980, in principle capable of reaching out to a population of 2.5 million.

This effort at community organization, initiated and conducted by the government, bypassed the traditional *kaifong* associations, which were considered incapable of representing the new generation that had appeared and grown up in the post-war period. The home base of these new community organizations were the housing estates in the new towns created by the public housing programme. Mutual aid committees were often initiated by social workers of the Housing Authority as an organized channel of communication. On the basis of this structure the District Administration Scheme was introduced in 1980. For the first time this opened up the political system to limited forms of political representation. It was to become the basis for the introduction of a process of political democratization in the 1980s and 1990s. By combining social reform and limited citizen participation, MacLehose had introduced a form of social democracy at the grassroots level through the vehicle of a public housing programme based largely on new towns. In so doing he had indelibly grafted the public housing system into the political fabric of Hong Kong society.

Income Distribution Effects

On a day-to-day basis, politics deals primarily with issues of distribution. The public housing programme is without a doubt the largest income redistribution programme in Hong Kong. We have seen earlier that the income distribution of renters in public housing was not very different from that of renters in private housing in 1976. Did the expansion of the public housing programme in the 1970s and 1980s change this?

Using data from the 1976 By-Census, the 1981 Census, the 1986 By-Census, and the 1991 Census of population, we are able to compare the income distribution of households in the public rental housing programme with those living in private rental housing. In Table 3.4 we report the percentage of households by decile (10%) income groups. The numbers are tabulated separately for private and public housing tenants for each of the census or by-census years. The decile income groups are defined using the full sample of all households in each year and applied to the population of public and private tenants. The income brackets obviously are not the same for the different years.

The figures show that with the exception of the top 10% of the income group, there are proportionately more households in low-income brackets among private tenants than among public housing tenants.. This suggests that public housing tenants tend to be less well-off than private tenants across all income groups, except for those at the very top of the income ladder. This is true for all years. From 1976 to 1986 there was a trend for private housing tenants to gravitate towards lower-income brackets, although the trend was reversed in 1991. From 1976 to 1986 the income distribution of public housing tenants remained fairly stable; however, there was a slight gravitation towards lower-income brackets in 1991.

Table 3.4

Percentage of Public and Private Tenant Households by Income Brackets, 1976–91

Income Bracket	Public Tenants				Private Tenants			
	1976	1981	1986	1991	1976	1981	1986	1991
Bottom 10%	8.25	9.03	6.88	9.60	9.67	11.30	14.17	13.24
2nd 10%	9.03	8.79	9.48	12.03	11.03	12.51	14.36	14.29
3rd 10%	10.31	10.07	11.65	12.91	10.75	11.74	11.78	11.30
4th 10%	11.37	11.28	12.83	13.16	10.19	10.73	9.87	9.64
5th 10%	11.81	11.68	12.39	12.61	10.26	10.01	9.64	8.35
6th 10%	11.54	11.35	12.09	11.32	10.01	10.04	8.91	7.73
7th 10%	12.25	11.65	11.74	10.01	9.39	8.91	8.04	8.01
8th 10%	11.47	11.15	10.63	8.85	9.26	8.66	7.28	6.84
9th 10%	10.00	10.25	8.89	7.09	9.21	7.97	7.31	7.22
Top 10%	3.98	4.75	3.42	2.42	10.23	8.14	8.64	13.38
All Brackets	100	100	100	100	100	100	100	100
No. of Households	34,058	20,161	72,769	28,552	32,054	17,263	39,032	10,921

Source: Estimated from population census data (various years).
Note: The income brackets are different from year to year, but are applied the same for both public and private renters in any given year. The income brackets are constructed by distributing an equal number of households, i.e., 10% of the households, into each income bracket using the sample of *all* households in that year.

It is evident that the public housing programme had failed to systematically benefit those who were really poor. Increasingly, the public housing programme appeared to exist primarily for those public housing tenants who were already privileged to be in the programme rather than to help those private tenants who were among the very disadvantaged. Given that political representation at the grassroots level was based largely on the political constituency of public housing tenants, the basic structure for redistributive politics to occur was already in place.

The Economic Effects

The economic consequences of MacLehose's housing programme were equally far-reaching. By pushing the public housing scheme to develop new towns and to grow to encompass half the population of Hong Kong, he altered not only the physical landscape of the territory but also the economic allocation of resources with wide-ranging effects on the life and activities of every resident and business. Let me explain how this is the case.

Over the years, the most important criteria used to measure the housing needs of the community has been the degree of sharing within a housing unit. This measure is obtained by dividing the number of household by the number of housing units. The planning assumption is that a shortage of housing is indicated when the degree of sharing is greater than one. Are we then to assume that there is no shortage when the degree of sharing equals one? The problem with this planning criteria is that it totally ignores the role of prices in determining shortages. It also fails to take into account the fact that housing units differ in many respects such as surface area, location, year of completion, building cost, and other attributes of housing accommodation, like tenure.

Consider the difference between public and private housing units. Public housing units can be further classified broadly into rental units and owner-occupied units. The average sizes of rental units and owner-occupied units in the public sector differ greatly. Table 3.5 shows that between 1982 and 1996 the average size of rental units increased from 24.58 to 30.85 square metres, and for owner-occupied units it increased from 52.24 to 55.10 square metres. It is obvious that adding together rental and owner-occupied units would not be an appropriate way by which to arrive at the total supply of public housing units.

There is also a great difference in the average size of private residential units and public housing units. Table 3.5 shows that the average size of the stock of private residential units has stayed remarkably stable over time, at about 55 square metres. Although the average size of the private units completed each year has been rising, it has had little impact on the average size of the total stock.

A public owner-occupied unit is about the same size as a private housing unit. A public rental unit is about 60% of the size of the average private housing unit. It is important to note two other relevant points. First, most public housing units are on average of

50   Chapter 3

Table 3.5
Residential Housing: Average Size (Square Metre)

Year	Private Housing		Public Housing	
	Net Stock	Flow Supply	Rental	Owner Occupied
1978		49.77	21.40	51.54
1979		49.20	22.52	51.55
1980		50.58	23.12	51.34
1981		53.98	23.72	51.47
1982		56.68	24.58	52.24
1983	55.65	60.64	24.93	53.82
1984	55.19	43.37	24.48	52.21
1985	54.58	43.68	24.53	51.77
1986	54.32	50.42	27.52	51.45
1987	54.23	53.85	25.38	51.93
1988	54.44	58.36	25.81	51.96
1989	54.73	61.09	27.73	52.16
1990	54.78	57.41	28.27	52.39
1991	54.85	59.90	28.22	52.84
1992	54.79	53.75	28.53	53.21
1993	54.73	54.18	29.20	53.72
1994	54.57	56.11	29.86	54.11
1995	55.74	63.20	30.03	54.80
1996	55.94	65.40	30.85	55.10

Source: Wong (1998).

lower quality. Second, almost all public housing units are governed by tenancy agreements and terms of ownership that impose severe limits on tenant mobility and asset transferability, so that public and private units are far from being perfect substitutes. It is clear that the typical public rental unit is significantly inferior to a private unit.

Since the distribution of income among tenants in the public and private housing sectors are not too different, therefore, their respective demands for housing cannot be too different, either. This implies that there must be serious distortion in the pattern of housing consumption. The distortion stems from a number of factors. First, a large number of public housing units are too small to meet the housing aspirations of the vast majority of the tenants who occupy them. Second, the unit may be in an inconvenient location. Third, the quality of the unit and of the neighbourhood may be sub-optimal. Fourth, the quality of management and maintenance work may differ from tenant aspirations and may be complicated by neighbour effects.

The economic inefficiencies of the public housing programme are not limited to the distortions in housing consumption alone. There are other forms of inefficiencies. First, residents in public housing differ significantly from those in private units in their freedom to change their place of residence. There is no market for public housing units. A public housing tenant who wishes to move literally has to trade his unit with another public housing tenant who wishes to do the same. The matching process is further complicated by the fact that side payments are difficult to arrange. This is an awkward form of bartering that simply cannot be efficient. It is well known that the turnover rate among public tenants is low. A tenant who joins the public housing programme would literally have to adjust his entire life and career pattern to accommodate his housing decision. Whether he works and his place of employment, whether his spouse works and her place of employment, where his children go to school, and so on, would all be dependent on this decision, unless he and his family were willing to put up with huge transportation costs. The human and economic costs that are incurred when over one-third of the population is tied down in this way are enormous. These costs are multiplied by the fact that most public housing estates are often located in far-off areas in the New Territories, where the new towns were developed.

Third, the concept of a self-contained new town with a mix of activities and facilities simply never worked. The idea that one could plan such new towns defies economic logic and fails to appreciate how market forces work. Economic activities tend to have huge agglomeration effects in terms of where they are located. While households can be enticed to live in inconveniently located public housing estates by offering them cheap rents, it is far more difficult to justify offering subsidies to businesses and factories to relocate to the remote new towns in a free-market economy. The outcome of these two different forces was to turn the new towns into primarily residential areas without economic activities and job opportunities. The distance between people's residences and their places of employment increased. The transportation system was overloaded, and parents and children had to endure arduous daily commutes to get to work and school.

Fourth, although the new towns were provisioned with new schools so that children could avoid long and tiring commutes every day, the government could not mandate quality education overnight. It was not simply a problem of providing a fair allocation of educational resources. The real problem was how to attract high-quality and motivated teachers to work in the new towns. Since a high-quality education in the new towns could not be assured, some parents preferred to have their children commute long distances to school. One wonders if the egalitarianism that spread through Hong Kong's school system in the 1970s resulting in common pay scales for all teachers and the introduction of a computerized system of allocation of school places by residence district were also by-products of the public housing programme. The resulting uniformity of the education system probably wrecked the incentives system for both teachers and students. If this is so, then the long-term cost of the public housing programme would probably have to include the erosion of educational standards that has been the focus of much public attention in recent years. These speculations are the proper subject of another study, and it is better to cease dwelling on them here.

As we shall see later, the economic inefficiencies of the public housing programme have been enormous. These inefficiencies stem from two sources. First, there are the inefficiencies of the public housing programme, and second, there are spill-over effects into other areas, which lead to other sources of inefficiency. In chapter 5, we attempt to estimate the social cost to society of the public rental housing programme. It is not possible to estimate all the inefficiencies, but those that can be estimated are sufficient to cause public alarm.

CHAPTER 4

Home Ownership and Public Housing Reforms: From 1984 to the Present

Throughout the 1980s and 1990s the demand for better housing rose among both private and public housing tenants as economic conditions continue to improve following the opening of China after 1979. In the private sector property prices rose dramatically from 1983 onwards. The rapid growth in housing demand and the slow growth of new supply drove property prices to astronomical heights. Table 4.1 presents some evidence of the phenomenal increase in real property prices and the sluggishness of housing supply. An in depth analysis of the factors underlying these events can be found in Wong (1992) and Wong, Liu and Siu (1993) and Siu, Wong and Liu (1996).

The unsatisfied demand was most acutely felt in the public sector. One important reason for this was that housing conditions in the public sector were decidedly inferior to those in the private sector. The situation was made worse by the fact that there was little difference in the household income levels of public and private tenants. The gap between aspirations and reality was enormous. It soon became apparent that it was no longer possible to accommodate the population's diverse housing needs through a monolithic public housing programme. Even redeveloping the early Mark I and Mark II resettlement housing estates and replacing them with better-quality public rental housing units was proving to be inadequate.

Chapter 4

Table 4.1
Property Price, Inflation and Private Housing Supply, 1980–97

Year	Inflation Rate		Private Domestic Units Built (as of the year end)	Private Housing Nominal Price Inflation Rate (year end to year end)
	CPIA (%)	Composite Price Index (%)		
1980	15.5	15.3	24,995	38.01
1981	15.4	14.3	34,475	5.08
1982	10.5	10.9	23,900	−18.52
1983	9.9	10.0	21,620	−13.44
1984	8.1	8.6	22,270	−1.94
1985	3.2	3.5	29,875	18.80
1986	2.8	3.8	34,105	9.80
1987	5.5	5.7	34,375	19.64
1988	7.6	7.0	34,470	31.34
1989	10.1	10.3	36,485	17.05
1990	9.8	10.2	29,400	14.56
1991	12.0	11.6	33,380	55.08
1992	9.4	9.6	26,222	18.58
1993	8.5	8.8	27,673	15.67
1994	8.1	8.8	34,173	15.54
1995	8.7	9.1	22,621	−10.00
1996	6.0	6.3	19,875	26.44
1997	5.8	5.9	18,200	40.83#

Sources: Census and Statistics Department, *Monthly Digest of Statistics* (various years). Rating and Valuation Department, *Hong Kong Property Review* (various years)

Note: # provisional figure

The new satellite towns turned into huge housing estates. The public housing tenants — a legacy of the MacLehose reforms — in these communities were politically well organized and were soon pressing ever more effectively for enhanced housing benefits. Meanwhile, public perception that public housing tenants were predominantly poor was changing. Previously, the public had conveniently assumed this to be the case, but it was beginning to become more and more clear that many of those living in public housing estates were in fact quite well off.

The study conducted by Wong and Liu (1988) was probably the first to systematically demonstrate this. Many well-publicized cases of well-off tenants who continued to occupy the heavily subsidized public housing units at the expense of other more financially deserving families were beginning to change public sentiment about the appropriateness of the existing policies.

Against this background the Housing Authority began to realign its priorities and the housing policy instruments. The new initiatives targeted different housing resources for groups with different needs. The Home Ownership Scheme (HOS) and the Private Sector Participation Scheme (PSPS) were aimed at the so-called "sandwich classes"; the segment of society too well off to qualify for public rental housing but unable to afford private housing. Over time, preferential treatment in the allocation of HOS and PSPS units was also introduced to encourage well-off public housing tenants to relinquish their units. This was done in the hope of reducing the long waiting list for public housing. In addition, a punitive "double rent" policy was also introduced to encourage well-off tenants in the public housing programme to give up their units.

The changing public housing programme reflected the evolving housing demands of a more affluent and increasingly pluralistic society. In the process the government and the Housing Authority began to assume a new and expanded role as the major provider of housing not only for families in hardship situations or without proper shelter but also for a broad spectrum of the middle income class.

In the first half of the 1990s inflation rates soared to double digit levels as a result of the structural transformation that took place following the expansion and migration of manufacturing industries across the border into south China. Private property prices skyrocketed, and many private sector tenants felt aggrieved as their hopes of becoming homeowners appeared to fall through. They were soon lobbying the government for new subsidies. The government introduced a new subsidized home-loan scheme for these "new sandwich classes". They fell into this category because their incomes disqualified them from applying for HOS and PSPS housing but at the same time were too low to allow them to purchase private housing. The Housing Society, which had fallen into decline after the 1950s, was revived with the introduction of the subsidized loan schemes for the new sandwich classes.

An important part of the enlarged function of the Housing Authority — and more recently of the Housing Society — is its role in providing home ownership units. The home ownership schemes also provided the Housing Authority with huge surpluses from profitable sales as a result of their access to land provided by government at nominal prices. The availability of ready financial resources provided the Housing Authority considerable freedom to pursue its own housing mandate.

By assuming responsibility for developing housing for more than just low-income families and displaced squatters, the Housing Authority set an agenda that would lead to its domination, similar in scope and scale to that of the Housing Development Board in Singapore, of the entire housing market.

New Policy Initiatives

The new housing policy was first introduced in the Housing Authority consultative document, *A Review of Public Housing Allocation Policies* (1984), and subsequently developed in a series of official documents. The enlarged role of the Housing Authority is explicit in various policy statements detailed in the *Long Term Housing Strategy* (1987), the *Mid-Term Review of the Long Term Housing Strategy* (1993), and the *Long Term Housing Strategy Review* (1997a).

The Housing Authority was reorganized on 1 April 1988 and was given autonomy and a separate financial identity in order to deal with the goals set out under the government's long-term housing strategy, while the government continued to commit to providing necessary funds to meet such goals.

More important, the 1987 review recommended a set of proposals that was to lead to a major transformation within the public sector resulting in the shift from public rental housing to home ownership. It was envisaged, by the year 2001 combined private and public sector home ownership will increase from 40% of the total housing stock to 59%, while the public rental sector will decline accordingly, from 40% of the total housing stock to 32% (*Mid-Term Review of the Long Term Housing Strategy*, p. 66). Although the government will still be responsible for about one-third of Hong Kong's residents through the public rental sector, the new housing policy aims at giving the future populace a stake in real estate property either through public provision or through the private market.

The 1987 review also emphasized the role of the private sector in a very specific way. According to some projections made in this document, the private sector was to represent about 54% of the housing stock in 2001. In other words, after a lengthy developmental process, the private sector would begin to gradually regain its relative dominance in the housing market. This was to be achieved primarily through the gradual devolution of public sector home ownership units into the private sector.

The main implication of the proposals was the public sector's even larger role in the developmental process. The creators of the proposal envisioned the public sector as being entrusted primarily with the task of increasing home ownership, since the strategy relied mainly on public provision rather than on private supply. The government has continued to endorse this approach in subsequent projections including the most recent one in 1997, which has also been supported by the new Government of the Hong Kong Special Administrative Region that came into office on 1 July 1997.

According to the government's 1997 review, in the period 1995–96 to 2000–01 an additional 85,000 housing units will be required each year, 54,000 of which will be supplied by the public sector. For the period 2001–02 to 2005–06, a total of 73,000 units will be supplied each year, 39,000 of which will be supplied by the public sector. These figures imply that the public sector's role in terms of housing will become even larger in the coming years. With some modifications, updating, and further elaboration of details, these proposals were incorporated into the policy address delivered by the Chief Executive of the Special Administrative Region, Mr. Tung Chee Hwa, at the Provisional Legislative Council meeting on 8 October 1997.

For a chronological account of the various policy initiatives introduced in these documents see Appendix 1: Major Events. These documents summarized the housing policy's main lines that were implemented in the 1980s. The new policy orientation can be summarized in six major policy changes.

Accommodating Tenant Demands

First, the housing policy changed by becoming more receptive to the demands of public housing tenants. The policy decision-making process of the Housing Authority was partially opened up to admit leaders of tenants and grass-roots organizations into various levels of the Authority's decision-making hierarchy.

Three specific tenant demands were accepted. First, small households (of one or two persons) were made eligible to be permanent public housing units tenants. The result was to expand the eligibility criteria to unmarried individuals and young married couples. The waiting list was thereby further lengthened.

Next, squatters became eligible for rehousing programmes, and not only those in settlements designated for redevelopment and clearance. This too expanded the waiting list and encouraged more households to become squatters.

The last demand accepted was that the spouse of one married child was allowed to be an additional tenant in the parents' flat. This effectively permitted a partial or limited transfer of the claim to public housing entitlements from one generation to the next. The significance of this policy was that it made a public housing entitlement a quasi-permanent claim against the government. The value of the entitlement to the household was of course enhanced. The value would have been even greater if the government had been perceived to be committed to a policy of redeveloping and upgrading the quality of the housing stock, a policy which the Housing Authority adopted in the 1970s.

Redevelopment of Public Housing Estates

Second, a major policy decision to expand the scope of the public housing redevelopment programme to include all housing estates built in the 1950s and 1960s went into effect. In one stroke, the government committed itself to redeveloping Mark I, II, III, IV, V, and VI resettlement estates. The generosity of this commitment exceeded the expectations of the tenants, who had not requested the redevelopment of Mark V and VI estates. This policy clearly signaled to tenants that the government was making a firm commitment to upgrade the quality of housing for the existing tenants and that it was therefore in their interest to stay in the programme.

Raising Public Housing Rents

Third, public housing rents went up. After years of neglect the Authority decided to review and formulate a set of new criteria for determining public housing rents. A 1984 survey showed that household income had grown by 97% in constant price terms, while public housing rents had decreased by 7% in real terms. Although rents were reviewed biennially, they had failed to keep pace with either inflation or with tenants' real income growth. According to census figures, the average rent to income ratio of public housing tenants was 7% in 1981 and 9.6[1] in 1991. Rents were originally set on the basis of a number of factors that took into account tenants' affordability levels, comparative estate values, government rates, inflation, and management and maintenance costs. It was agreed that rent should be set so as not to exceed 15% of the median income of tenant households.

An ad hoc committee set up to review "Rent Policy and Allocation Standards" issued a report in December 1990. The report found that the median rent to income ratio (MRIR) ranged from 5.2% to 10.6% for public tenant households. The overall median rent to income ratio upon intake of public housing was 14.3% in 1988–89, but the ratio tended to decrease after the household had joined the programme, because household incomes was rising faster than rents were. Rents in public housing estates were 17% to 45% of comparable units in the private sector.[2] In 1990 rents were set at $25.60 per square metre, or about 30% of the market value for new flats in estates with the best location and facilities.

The ad hoc committee also found that tenants in general preferred larger flats. Some 95% of the lower-income applicants in the period April 1988 to September 1989 indicated a willingness to pay higher rents for larger units. The committee recommended that public tenants be offered a choice between the current allocation standard of 5.5 m^2 per person and a new standard of 7.7 m^2 per person. Rents were to be set so that the median rent-to-income ratio did not exceed 15% for the smaller unit and 18.5% for the larger unit when the tenants first move into public housing.

Double Rent Policy

Fourth, the double rent policy targeted at well-off public housing tenants was introduced. The idea was first proposed in the Green Paper entitled *Housing Subsidy to Tenants of Public Housing* issued in August 1985. In the following year the Housing Authority adopted the double rent policy to reduce the amount of subsidy to public housing tenants and to encourage home ownership. The intention was to reallocate the housing units relinquished by well-off tenants to those on the waiting list. Aside from making the use of these housing resources more equitable, another objective of the Green Paper was to cap the growth of the public housing programme by inducing more well-off tenants to surrender their units for allocation to households on the waiting list.

Households whose total income exceeded the income limit on the public housing waiting list by 100% were considered well off. Households that had been in the public housing programme for more than ten years would have to be means tested in order to be exempted from the double rent policy. The double rent policy was to be implemented in stages. It first dealt with tenants who had been in the programme for twenty-two years or more and will later extend to cover all tenants of more than ten years. Assessments carried out in 1990 required 18,700 households that had been living in public housing for fourteen to eighteen years and another 3,400 households that are due for biennial income review to pay double rent from 1 April 1990. Needless to say, the policy was extremely unpopular with public housing tenants. Many tenants who were not immediately affected were also opposed to the double rent policy because they expect to be adversely affected in the future.

Promoting Home Ownership

Fifth, the emphasis on home ownership was renewed. The main initiatives were the implementation of the HOS and PSPS schemes described in the previous section. The HOS units were very popular. By 1986 some 50,000 units had been sold; half of them went to previous occupants of rental public housing. Over time the Housing Authority increasingly gave priority in the allocation of HOS units to public housing tenants in a race to shorten the public rental housing waiting list. By 1996, some 224,196 units of HOS flats have been built and 12.2% of all households were occupying HOS flats. In addition, the Home Purchase Loan Scheme (HPLS) was introduced in 1987 to offer low-interest loans on down payments to public housing tenants to encourage them to purchase private sector flats.

Acceptance of Squatter Settlements

Sixth, the long-term existence of squatter settlements was accepted. A number of programmes were implemented to improve sites and services in these settlements. The decision was a positive one, and it halted the perverse incentives that were created by the long-standing policy to resettle squatters in the mistaken belief that squatter settlements could eventually be cleared. Hong Kong's past record in the area of resettlement has demonstrated that this is an inconsistent and self-defeating policy in the face of sustained immigration and overcrowding in private housing. Indeed, in 1997 the government of Mr. Tung Chee Hwa was still announcing new pledges to clear squatter settlements and rehouse occupants in Temporary Housing Areas.

The attempt to shorten the queue for public housing units and to entice well-off public housing tenants to join the HOS, PSPS, and HPLS schemes was compromised by the conflicting signals of the six policy changes we have discussed. The first and second policy measures had the effect of lengthening the queue, and the third, fourth, and fifth measures had the opposite effect. That these policies are inconsistent is not surprising. They are symptomatic of the difficulties in, if not the impossibility of, designing coherent housing policies with multiple objectives and implementing them through a non-market process.

The diverse housing needs of an increasingly middle-class society are not easily compartmentalized into neat boxes to be separately targeted by specific housing policy measures. The tendency for these measures to have unintended spillover effects into adjacent boxes is to be expected because regulation-based measures do not possess the discerning power of the market, with its ability to individualize the effects specifically to each household.

Subsidized Home Ownership

By the mid-1970s the economy was recovering from the earlier economic recession. Housing prices and rents were soon on the rise. As a consequence, a substantial group of middle-income households found themselves unable to afford a flat on the open market. The group's monthly incomes were also above the eligibility limits for public rental housing. In 1976 the Housing Authority therefore decided to introduce the subsidized Home Ownership Scheme.

Under the scheme, the government was to build flats for purchase by families from the private sector with incomes between $3,500 and $5,000 per month. Since then income eligibility limits have been periodically revised. The decision to help these households represents an unusual step on the government's part. In the 1950s its housing policy had ceased to assist middle-income households. Early initiatives were taken over by the Housing Society, whose role in providing public housing had become almost negligible in the interim two or more decades.

The government decision to provide housing support for middle-income households can be understood from several perspectives. First, as Hong Kong society evolved from a largely immigrant one into a community of permanent residents, rent-seeking activities became more politically effective. Rising affluence and growing political pluralism encouraged participation in public affairs and precipitated a greater demand for public sector activity and intervention. Second, the earlier public housing programmes had created a situation in which substantial housing benefits were given to large segments of society without any means tests. The case for providing subsidies to those in the private sector became difficult to refuse because their economic circumstances were not very different from those of many well-off public housing tenants. Third, the influence of public housing tenants on the public policy process is particularly strong because of their ability to institutionalize their political activity. These political economy effects have contributed to and facilitated the propensity of the public sector to expand in the housing area.

Tenants in public rental housing units were subsequently also eligible to apply for flats in the HOS without income restriction on the condition that they give up tenancy of their rental flat upon moving into a HOS unit. One of the objectives of the scheme was obviously to move those households who could afford the HOS units out of the public rental housing programme in order to free some of these units for applicants on the waiting list.

In 1976 the PSPS supplemented the HOS to increase flat production. Sites were offered for sale to private real estate developers on the condition that the flats produced be sold at fixed prices to purchasers nominated by the government. The criteria of eligibility were the same as were those for HOS flats. In addition, the PSPS scheme aimed to tap the creative role of private developers in housing construction. The PSPS scheme was unfortunately a major disappointment for the Housing Authority in this respect.

The Authority had hoped that private sector participation would enhance the quality of the units built. This did not happen, however, and many occupants complained incessantly about the poor quality of and defects in the construction and finishing work. Since private developers had to sell the units at government-determined prices, it was entirely in their interest to minimize costs as much as they could. As is to be expected, it was not too difficult for them to do this, because the Housing Authority's incentive to compulsively monitor the work of private developers was poor.

In his policy address, Mr. Tung Chee Hwa more recently proposed the implementation of a pilot scheme to tender selected sites, subject to the requirement that the developer hand over at least 30% of the flats built to the government. The units would then be sold to eligible purchasers at designated prices. A crucial issue here is that of whether the 30% of the units to be handed over to the government will be pre-designated or selected after the units have been completed.

To avoid the perverse incentive effects present in the PSPS, the developer must not know until after the units are completed which specific units will be handed over to the government. It is, however, desirable for government and the developers to agree at the outset on a rule to decide how to select the units. This new policy will consequently create mixed neighbourhood developments and will probably have a negative effect on the sales prices of the units and on the bid values for these sites. It will also make explicit the subsidy provided by the government to eligible home purchasers. The sales prices or the mechanism for setting sales prices of units to be handed over to the government must be known to the developers at the outset; otherwise they would not be able to set sales prices for their own units and to set bid values for the site. The details of these arrangements and the way in which uncertainty is to be managed will be important and will have various incentive effects. Ambiguities in the contract may lead to renegotiations between the government and developers after the units have been completed. This will create uncertainty and affect both sales prices and bid values.

The price of flats in HOS and PSPS was originally set to cover building costs, land value, overhead, and administrative charges. To curb reselling of subsidized units on the free market for speculative profit, purchasers were not allowed to resell their flats within the first five years of ownership. But, in September 1981, by which time building costs and land values sharply escalated since the initial phase was completed in 1978, the government decided to exclude the value of land from flat prices, although an element of cost was retained to cover the cost of land formation. With the price reductions, the Housing Authority considered it necessary to introduce more stringent measures to curb speculative reselling.

The resale conditions for HOS and PSPS flats were revised. According to the new guidelines, in the first five years flats may be resold only to the Housing Authority at the original selling price. During the second five-year period, flats may be resold only to the Authority at a price related to other similar HOS flats being offered for sale at that time. After ten years of occupation, flats may be resold either to the Authority, as in the second five-year period, or on the open market, with payment to the government of the updated value of the original discount that can be attributed to market forces.

Since 1985 eligibility for HOS units has been extended to public housing waiting list applicants. HOS flats are sold at 25% to 40% below market value, depending on market conditions, so as to reach the lower middle-income target groups. To curb speculation, purchasers are subject to the same reselling restrictions.

Since the Housing Authority put limitations on the resale options, the HOS and PSPS schemes have become less attractive to tenants in the public housing programme. The advantage of the two schemes was that they offered the choice of an improved unit in a better location, but to get such a unit tenants had to pay a higher price. Unless property prices appreciated substantially, the prospect of realizing significant capital gains through the sale of the unit would be limited.

The attempt to convince well-off tenants to give up their public housing units was therefore not always successful. Many public housing units remained "frozen". To make things worse, many public housing tenants were increasingly successful in lobbying to legitimize the transfer of public housing tenancy rights to their descendants. From the point of view of the public housing tenant, owning a home that entailed financial outlays at the outset and that could not be transferred for many years could be inferior to having a permanent claim to public housing tenancy rights. Such claims were almost risk free, and they could appreciate over time if the government were perceived to be committed to a policy of replacing current buildings with better structures.

In a bid to encourage more public housing tenants to give up their tenancies, to reduce the length of the waiting list, and to encourage home ownership, in 1997 the Housing Authority decided to allow HOS units to be sold to public housing tenants and those on the waiting list. HOS occupants are now free to sell their units to eligible buyers three years after they made their initial purchase at prices to be determined on the market. In 1997 the total number of HOS units that could be sold after the three-year limit was more than 100,000. Public housing tenants were required to give up their tenancies upon buying these HOS units. Occupants of these HOS units were not required to pay a land premium to the Housing Authority when the units were sold to eligible buyers. The initiative to create a secondary market in HOS units among eligible purchasers was a popular one and represented a useful step in enhancing the circulation of otherwise frozen HOS and public rental housing units.

The Housing Authority as a Unique Institution

Today, the Housing Authority finds itself embroiled in the management of conflicting political demands and housing objectives. There is first a large group of aspiring homeowners in the private sector that cannot afford to buy homes on the open market. There is a second group of private renters who are eagerly waiting to join the public housing programme. There is also a third group of public housing renters who are not always willing to relinquish their public housing units unless the terms are decidedly in their favour. In addition, the Housing Authority wishes to cap the size of the public housing programme at its present level. The policy decision-making process has become highly politicized. The fact that today some two-thirds of HOS units are allocated to public housing tenants (Green Form applicants) and only one-third to private housing tenants (White Form applicants) is evidence of the power of the incumbents in making their preferences prevail.

Although it is easy to think of the HOS and PSPS schemes as attempts to enlarge the private housing sector through home ownership, this will in fact only be realized in the long run. Given resale restrictions, most of the units are not available on the private market until ten years after their purchase. Moreover, because of resale restrictions, these units are not perceived by their occupants as being bona fide privately owned. The Housing Authority is also heavily involved in providing and managing these units. It is therefore more appropriate to consider the HOS and PSPS schemes to be publicly managed home ownership programmes in which property rights in the housing units are jointly owned by the occupant and the Authority. The housing units will become fully private after a ten-year period.

Perhaps one of the most important consequences of the HOS and PSPS schemes was that it provided the Housing Authority with very large surpluses from the sale of flats. Sales prices of the units were related to market levels, but land obtained from the government was essentially free except for the payment of the cost of development. As land values rose and the HOS and PSPS schemes grew, the Housing Authority became enormously well funded. The financial pressures for cutting costs were reduced. There was now considerable room to cross-subsidize the administrative and redevelopment expenses of rental units using proceeds from the sale of ownership units. The Authority also provided the necessary funding for operating various loan schemes to tenants.

The Housing Authority is a unique bureaucracy that, having been assured of funding through its access to valuable land at cheap prices, is financially free to define and implement its own plans in many ways. A mechanism has been devised whereby the provision of better-quality housing units can be financially assured almost indefinitely. This is a severe threat to the development of the private housing sector, as developers continue to move to higher-priced markets to avoid competing directly with the Housing Authority. Many small developers today have become construction companies working on various public sector projects.

Selling Public Rental Housing

The difficulties of operating a huge public housing programme with a reasonable degree of coherence and efficiency have also led some government policy thinkers to question the desirability of relying heavily upon public provision to solve housing issues.

The Housing Authority's most interesting initiative by far has been to sell public housing units to existing tenants. In 1990 it proposed a limited programme through which to sell some of its public housing units to sitting tenants. On 18 October 1990 an ad hoc committee of the Housing Authority issued a pamphlet detailing its views on how to implement the experimental proposal. Some 3,000 to 4,000 units from a number of public housing estates about five years old were selected as part of a pilot plan. Each tenant in these estates was offered the choice of buying his or her flat at a discount off the imputed market rent. The offer was, however, conditional on more than 50% of the tenants in a block opting to buy; otherwise there would be no sale.

The 50% trigger threshold was chosen to allow the Housing Authority to withdraw from the management of sold blocks. The committee envisaged that management problems in the mixed tenure situation would arise as a result of the divergence of interest between owner/occupiers and tenants. To protect the value of their investments, owner occupants were expected to be more willing than public housing tenants would be to spend resources to have their buildings properly maintained. With a 50% cut-off point, the Authority assumed that it would be able to play the role of a passive minority owner and simply follow the dictate of the majority owners.

This policy was greeted with some apprehension. Various grass-roots organizations concerned with public housing had an immediate negative reaction. They accused the government of failing to live up to its commitment to house the poor. Public housing tenants, on the other hand, were more concerned with the price at which the government would sell the units. When the plan took on its final form in 1991, however, few tenants accepted the offer, even though the units were being offered at 55% of the estimated market price. A subsequent attempt to sell the units at 30% of the market price in October 1992 with a trigger threshold of 30% was not approved by the Executive Council.

So, can we say that privatization of public housing has been tried and that it failed? The answer is no. The real reason that tenants refused to accept the Housing Authority's offer is simple: severe limitations imposed on resale rights mean that the tenant turned owner does not have exclusive right over his or her property.[3] The resale limitations are similar to those imposed on the sale of HOS flats. An asset with such resale restrictions can only be sold at a deep discount to its market value. Tenants are unwilling to pay a mortgage far higher than their subsidized rent if they are not going to be able to reap any capital gain when they sell the asset.

More important, given these resale restrictions, a buyer receives no compensation for giving up his tenancy right. From the point of view of the public housing tenant, owning a home that entails financial outlays at the outset and whose transfer rights are restricted may be inferior to having a permanent claim to public housing tenancy rights. Such claims are almost risk free, and, as has been previously stated, their value may appreciate over time if the government is perceived to be committed to a policy of replacing current buildings with better structures. The initial offer to sell public housing units failed not because the price was not low enough, or because the tenants could not afford it, or because the quality of the units was not high enough. Tenants simply calculated that it was not worth trading a valuable permanent entitlement — cheap rent — for an asset whose market value was limited by transfer restrictions.

Siu (1990) points out that resale restrictions, though undesirable, are probably still acceptable to many public housing tenants. He cites as evidence the fact that the success rate of Green Form or public housing tenant applications for HOS flats was usually between 5% and 10%. In other words, he argues that large numbers of public housing tenants are eager to give up their public housing tenancy rights without compensation in order to join the HOS. It is, however, important to note that these large numbers are actually quite small compared with the entire stock of public housing tenants, and there is no reason to believe that they are concentrated in any individual public housing block.

It is critical to recognize that public housing is a form of welfare transfer-in-kind rather than a cash subsidy. Tenants have little choice with respect to location, size, and other housing characteristics when they take up units. One must either accept the offer extended or go back to the end of the queue and wait for an uncertain period until one is called again. Acceptance of a unit does not imply that one values it at its full market value; it only indicates that the rent is so low that one is willing to tolerate all the unpleasant and inconvenient aspects of accepting the offer. For example, if someone who works in Aberdeen, on the south side of Hong Kong Island, gets a public housing unit in Tuen Mun — a train, subway, and bus ride away, he will not value the unit as much as someone who works in Tuen Mun would. Therefore, unlike private housing units that are chosen freely, the subjective value of a public housing unit to the tenant may differ significantly from its market value.

Indeed, the most popular feature of the HOS scheme to public housing tenants is that it allows the tenant to choose where to reside. This option is not available in the proposed scheme to sell public housing units to the sitting tenant. The tenant turned occupant is still tied to his own unit. If he chooses to sell it, he may not be able to buy a similar unit elsewhere. His options are limited not only because he cannot obtain the capital gains from selling the unit, but also because the initial proposal to sell public housing units was a pilot scheme in which only a small number of units were involved. It was insufficient to create a market in ex-public housing units.

The key element necessary to allow privatization to succeed is therefore free transferability. If a unit can be freely transferred after the tenant acquires it, then an initial selling price set at 55% (subsequently revised to 30%) of the market price as originally proposed by the Housing Authority would be attractive. The tenant would have implicitly received a capital gain equal to 45% (or, correspondingly, 70%) of the value of the unit. One would be foolish not to accept such an offer. Banks would be willing to offer mortgages of up to 100% of the initial sale price, since they would have as security an asset whose value was substantially higher. There would be little need for even an initial down payment. The setting of an attractive selling price is important only insofar as there will be restrictions on the transfer rights.

It is fortunate that the Housing Bureau and the Housing Authority are once again looking to privatization as a solution to Hong Kong's housing problems. The recent policy address delivered by Mr. Tung Chee Hwa in October 1997 proposed the sale of 25,000 public housing units per year in the coming ten years. If the proposal succeeds this time it will re-create the market that was gradually destroyed over four long decades. To succeed, the proposal must go all the way: it must relax restrictions on resale options and implement the sales programme on a large scale. It is most unfortunate that the previous privatization attempt failed. Had it succeeded in 1991 the entire public housing population would have benefited enormously. They would have acquired an asset that would have helped them hedge against the high inflation rates that Hong Kong has experienced since then. They would all have become several times wealthier by now. The privatization of public housing is a step in the right direction and should be encouraged. For it to succeed, however, the government must act boldly. These issues will be taken up in greater detail in the final chapter.

Table 4.2
Recipient and Application Characteristics of the Home Purchase Loan Scheme (HPLS), 1988–98

Year	Annual Quota	Recipients		The total amount of HPL offered (in million)		Applications			
		No. of Recipients[1] Receiving Loans or Monthly Subsidies				No. and Percentage of Applications		Approved number and Percentage	
		Loan	Monthly Subsidy	Loan	Monthly Subsidy	Green Form White Form (%) (%)		Green Form White Form (%) (%)	
1988 / 89	2,500	557	n.a.	39.0	n.a.	3,178	n.a.	557	n.a.
1989 / 90	6,000	3,022	n.a.	332.4	n.a.	5,007(51)	4,768(49)	1,777(59)	1,245(41)
1990 / 91	3,000	2,935	n.a.	369.9	n.a.	3,304(54)	3,078(46)	1,800(61)	1,135(39)
1991 / 92	3,500	1,006	36	130.8	0.11	1,053(45)	1,288(55)	586(56)	456(44)
1992 / 93	1,500	167	102	25.1	2.16	314(33)	631(67)	140(52)	129(48)
1993 / 94	1,000	544	157	108.8	5.48	540(31)	1,221(69)	248(35)	453(65)
1994 / 95	1,500	758	135	221.4	9.72	799(27)	2,142(73)	355(40)	538(60)
1995 / 96	3,000	3,148	221	1,660.1	13.62	7,160(61)	4,539(39)	2,365(70)	1,004(30)
1996 / 97	7,000	5,377	421	2,888.0	29.62	8,336(65)	4,432(35)	4,070(70)	1,728(30)
1997 / 98[2] (as at 31 Aug 97)	4,500	1,728	150	881.4	18.45	1,002	n.a.	1,078	800

Source: Hong Kong Housing Authority.

Note: 1. Apart from the interest-free loan originally provided under the loan scheme, a monthly subsidy for mortgage repayment was introduced in 1991 as an additional option to assist the interested families to purchase their own domestic flats. Applicants may only choose either option.

2. The acceptance of White Form applications for 1997/98 has not been opened. n.a.=not available.

Subsidized Home Loan Schemes

The provision of interest-free subsidized loans to help public housing tenants buy private housing flats through the Home Purchase Loan Scheme (HPLS) was quite popular. The scheme was designed primarily to encourage public housing tenants to give up their public housing units, but waiting list applicants were also eligible. However, the scope and scale of the scheme was limited by the amount of funds available to the Housing Authority and determined by the level of housing prices prevailing in the private sector. In Table 4.2 various statistics of the HPLS are presented.

In 1988–89 a quota of 2,500 loans, of $70,000 each was announced; but by the end of the year, only 577 had been taken up. The poor response was attributed to the sharp escalation in private sector housing prices during the year, which eroded the value of the loan. The loan amount in 1989–90 was increased to $110,000. Some 6,000 quotas were set aside, and 3,022 were taken up. Over the years the HPLS have been enhanced periodically to catch up with housing price inflation. A monthly subsidy to help loan recipients to cover mortgage payments was also made available on a need basis. The total loans made have risen enormously over time. In 1996–97 a total of 5,377 loans were provided amounting to a sum equal to $2.89 billion. In the same period the total number of mortgage loans provided by the banks was 122,599 with a gross value of $189.86 billion. The Housing Authority was beginning to become a provider of home loans; a role which traditionally belonged almost exclusively to the banks.

In 1991 domestic property prices surged. Private tenants who were not eligible for subsidized public housing and HOS units saw their hopes of acquiring a unit dashed within the span of a few weeks. They could no longer afford to buy a unit at current prices, and this was unlikely to change in the foreseeable future, as property prices continued to rise.

Many legislators were urging the government to provide some form of subsidized relief to households in the so-called new sandwich class, whose interests had been hurt by double-digit

Table 4.3
Distribution of Households by Tenure Type, 1991

Tenure Type	Monthly Income		
	below $18,000	$18,000–$40,000	above $40,000
Owner Occupier	467,539	156,345	49,183
Tenant:	726,197	89,023	22,131
Public housing	513,105	58,002	3,142
Private housing	213,092	31,021	18,989
Employer Provided	32,575	10,849	9,261
Rent Free	15,071	1,323	575
All Types	1,241,382	257,540	81,150
(100%)	(78.6%)	(16.3%)	(5.1%)

Source: Wong (1992d)

inflation and escalating property prices. In 1991 this group was identified as comprising those with monthly household incomes between $18,000 and $40,000. The lower limit denotes the level of income above which a family is not eligible to apply for subsidized public housing and HOS units, and the upper limit denotes the level of income necessary to support mortgage payments for a small unit in the private sector at the time.

Based on this classification, 16.3% of all households are in the new sandwich class, according to figures from the 1991 Census of Population (see Table 4.3). The sandwich class is therefore in the top quintile of the household income distribution. In 1991 a family with two children with a monthly income of $30,000 had to pay the standard tax rate of 15% of total assessable income. If the same family had an income above $13,800 it would have had to pay taxes at the maximum 25% marginal rate until it reached the standard tax rate level.

Households in the "new sandwich class" are clearly those at the bottom of the high-income tax bracket whose interests have been hurt by inflation because real savings have been eroded. With double-digit inflation, real savings fall rapidly over time. The flight to property as an inflation hedge is a natural response. Households that do not own property will find their lifetime wealth position declining rapidly both in absolute and relative terms.

One could effectively hedge against the effect of asset price inflation on wealth erosion in the 1990s if one owned property. It was believed that private renters were particularly hard hit by inflation because they were not homeowners, and if they belonged to the new sandwich class they would not be eligible for subsidized public housing and HOS programs. Figures from Table 4.3 indicate that in 1991, 42.6% of households were homeowners, 36.3% lived in public rental housing, and 16.7% lived in private rental housing. Among private renters, 213,021 had incomes below $18,000, and 31,092 households were in the new sandwich class.

The government yielded to political pressure and decided to introduce a subsidized home purchase scheme for first-time home purchasers in the new sandwich class. The new initiative called for the spending of $2 billion to finance a discount home purchase scheme for 3,000 first-time home purchasers within three years. Given that there are about 30,000 such households, the government felt that it could assume responsibility for providing discounted loans to all private sector households in the new sandwich class over a period of ten years.

Interestingly, the number of applications for the sandwich class housing loan scheme, when it was implemented in 1993, was quite disappointing. In the first exercise a total of only 2,511 families put in a bid. This was only 6% of the estimated 40,000 eligible households. Commentators blamed bungled administrative arrangements and society's generally unhelpful attitude as presenting serious barriers to all but the most determined.[4]

In reality, the criteria was quite restrictive. Families had to have lived in Hong Kong for at least seven years, and family income had to fall between $20,001 and $40,000. Each household had to have at least three members. An applicant had not only to be living in a private rented flat, but no family member could have owned property in the previous two years. When all these criteria had been met, the eligible number of households was probably significantly less than the estimated 40,000. It is not evident that the remaining households would all want to be homeowners. Furthermore, if the units they bought were to be sold within three years, then the government loan would have to be repaid immediately. This also reduced the attractiveness of the scheme. In the subsequent years the scheme became more popular, largely because more families became eligible as inflation pushed more households into this income group.

Whether the government should spend resources to help the top quintile of the income distribution at the expense of the relatively poor members of society can be debated, but it is doubtful that the programme can be justified on equity grounds. Such a programme will also add to the existing economic inefficiencies of government interventions in the housing market. Interestingly, the programme was further extended in the first policy address delivered by Mr. Tung Chee Hwa. He proposed to increase the number of sandwich class housing flats that were to be built, raising the total to 50,000 units by 2006. He further proposed to introduce a new "Home Starter" loan scheme, over and above the existing sandwich class housing loan scheme. The new scheme would target first-time home buyers and would give 6,000 families a loan of $600,000 each in each of the next five years. The political clout and rent-seeking activities of the middle-income classes must not be underestimated.

Notes

1. It is reported that for 1996 the share of rent in household income among public renters has fallen to 8%.

2. Rates and management fees are typically included in public housing rental payments but excluded from private rental contracts.

3. I extensively analyze the failure of the initial privatization attempt in a series of articles I wrote more than five years ago. see Wong (1990, 1992a, 1992b, 1992c, 1992d) and Wong and Staley (1992). On 9 July 1992, I was also involved in extensive discussions with Sir David Akers-Jones and his colleagues on the subject in an effort to revive the privatization scheme. Sir David was then Chairman of the Housing Authority.

4. See Editorial, *South China Morning Post*, 4 September 1993.

CHAPTER 5

Economic Efficiency and Distribution of Benefits

Inefficiency of the Public Housing Programme

The public housing programme in Hong Kong provides an in-kind transfer to eligible households. Under this scheme, a household is allocated a flat on the basis of the Housing Authority's assessment of its housing requirements. The household is charged a rent that is about a quarter to a third of the market level. Tenants are given little choice with respect to location, size, and other characteristics of the housing unit they are assigned. The typical unit is built according to a standard set of designs that offers a limited range of choices. The flat provides the household with a stream of housing services.

A subsidy-in-kind does not allow the household to choose the housing unit it can select on the open market. Such a choice would only be available if the subsidy were in the form of a cash grant made through an income subsidy or a housing voucher that provided a rental subsidy.

The rent charged for public housing units is lower than the market level rent. The difference between the market rent and the rent charged by the government is considered the *gross subsidy* provided by the government to households. Contrary to what some people might think, the *gross subsidy* is the cost society has to pay. It is incorrect to measure the cost of the public housing programme as the sum of the construction cost of the buildings, the land formation cost, the interest cost, and the administrative and management cost, minus the rent charged by the Housing Authority.

Figure 5.1

**Effect of Public Housing Programme:
Increases housing consumption significantly
(when $H_m < H_c < H_s$)**

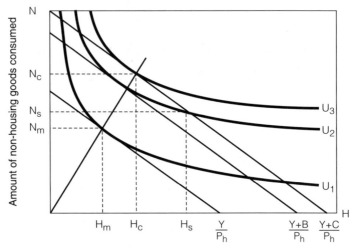

Amount of housing consumed

Notes: 1. U_1, U_2, U_3 are "indifference curves" with $U_1 < U_2 < U_3$. The tangent lines are the
               budget lines.
           2. H and N are respectively housing and non-housing goods consumed.
           3. Y is income, P_h is price of housing.
           4. B is unrestricted cash grant, C is gross subsidy under public housing.

From an economic point of view, the *gross subsidy* is the
opportunity cost to society of not using the land to develop market
housing and of renting out public housing units at the market rent.
If the subsidized rent is one-third of the market rent, then society is
providing the remaining two-thirds as a subsidy. In other words, the
subsidy provided by society is twice the subsidized rent.

Under the public housing programme, a household must stay in
the flat assigned it by the Housing Authority in order to obtain the
subsidy. Suppose the household were given an income or rental
subsidy equivalent in value to the *gross subsidy* spent on the public
housing programme. Would the household choose a private unit on
the open market that was similar to the flat assigned by the Housing

Authority? Most likely it would not. The private unit the household would choose could be either a better or a worse unit than the one provided by the Housing Authority. This difference in choice reflects an underlying economic inefficiency. In other words, given that society has decided to provide a housing subsidy, it would be better for the recipient if he or she could have the freedom to choose his or her preferred unit. To the extent that households have different preferences, it is inefficient to force them to consume exactly the same housing bundle. This is why economists believe that transfers-in-kind are inferior to cash transfers.

Empirical studies conducted in numerous countries demonstrate that public housing programmes of the sort that exists in Hong Kong are enormously inefficient and wasteful (see Aaron and Furstenberg 1971, Clemmer 1984, DeSalvo 1971, and Olsen and Barton 1983). Such programmes result in significant misallocation of resources and distortion of consumption patterns and may sometimes even worsen income distribution.

A Simple Theoretical Framework

In this section we develop a simple analysis to elucidate the nature and effects of the public housing programme from an economic standpoint. A more elaborate and technical discussion can be found in Wong and Liu (1988). Consider a household consuming only two things: housing services, H, and non-housing goods, N. In Figure 5.1 we have drawn several indifference curves for a household living in public housing. Along each indifference curve the household is equally satisfied with the different combinations of H and N. Higher indifference curves denote higher levels of satisfaction. In the absence of the public housing programme, a household with income Y will consume H_m units of housing services and N_m units of non-housing goods. If the price of each unit of H is P_h and the price of each unit of N is P, the household will spend its income on H and N subject to the budget constraint,

$$Y = P_h H_m + P N_m \, .$$

Under the public housing programme, the household has been offered and has accepted a dwelling unit providing H_s units of housing services. The household has to pay a total rent of R_s in order to occupy this unit. The remaining income is used to purchase N_s units of non-housing goods with

$$N_s = (Y - R_s) / P$$

where $R_s < P_h H_s$, and $N_s > N_m$. Note that the public housing programme does not shift or rotate the budget line. It merely adds an additional point (H_s, N_s) to the household's available set of opportunities in the choice of H and N.

The benefit to the household of joining the public housing programme is equivalent to receiving an unrestricted cash grant B that would keep the household equally satisfied. This is indicated in Figure 5.1 by the budget line that intersects the horizontal axis at $(Y + B) / P$ and is tangential to the indifference curve that passes through the point (H_s, N_s). One can think of this as providing an income supplement that is just enough to make the public housing tenant as well off as he or she would be under the current public housing programme. This amount can be considered the amount of *net benefit* received by the public housing tenant.

Suppose that instead of building public housing units, the government auctions off land to private developers who build private housing units. The proceeds of the land sales are transferred to tenants in the form of a cash grant. The government's true outlays would be the same because the cash grant would be equal to the *gross subsidy*.

In Figure 5.1 we have drawn another line passing through the consumption point under the public housing programme (H_s, N_s) and intersecting the horizontal axis at $(Y + C) / P_h$. The value of C is the *gross subsidy*. H_c and N_c are the units of housing services and non-housing goods that the household would have consumed had it been given an unrestricted cash grant equal to C instead of the public housing unit.

Note that C is the difference between the market value of the housing services and non-housing goods consumed by the household under the public housing programme and the household's initial income endowment. The market value of the public housing programme is C, but its value to the tenant is B. Since B < C, therefore, the household is better off with the cash grant, C. The above discussion shows that the amount of *net benefit* received by the households is less than the *gross subsidy* paid by the government. This is the rationale for economists' belief that cash grants are superior to transfers-in-kind.

We have shown that households will be better off if the subsidized public housing scheme is replaced by a cash grant in the form of an income subsidy scheme that will cost the government the same amount. The difference between the gross subsidy paid by the government and the *net benefit* received by households constitutes the wasted portion of government expenditure. This is the economic efficiency loss of operating the public housing programme as a transfer-in-kind scheme. The degree of the efficiency of the programme can be measured by the ratio B/C.

Note also that both the *gross subsidy* and the *net benefit* will rise if public housing rental subsidies are increased. Whether the degree of efficiency will be higher or lower depends on how *gross subsidies* and *net benefits* are differentially affected. In general, the efficiency will be higher at lower levels of household income and if the preference for housing consumption is weaker.

It is possible for the level of housing consumption under the public housing programme, H_s, to be less than what the household would choose to consume, H_c, if it were given an unrestricted cash grant, C. In Figure 5.2 we show how $H_s < H_c$ can occur. It is even possible for the household to be offered and to accept a dwelling unit that is worse than that which it would choose to occupy without any subsidy. This occurs if the rent charged is low enough that the loss in housing consumption is more than compensated for by the gain in non-housing consumption. In Figure 5.3 we show how $H_s < H_m$ can occur. This means that voluntary participation in the public housing programme does not imply that tenants necessarily consume more housing services than they would in the absence of the programme. As we shall demonstrate later, public

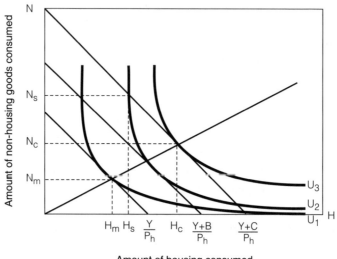

Figure 5.2

**Effect of Public Housing Programme:
Increases housing consumption moderately
(when $H_m < H_s < H_c$)**

Amount of housing consumed

housing tenants in Hong Kong actually consume less housing services than they would in the absence of the programme. Figures from Tables 3.4 and 3.5 together show the large differences in the size of housing units between the public and private sectors are not justified by the small differences in household income between the two.

Empirical Results

The theoretical framework discussed in the previous section is implemented using a model developed in Wong and Liu (1988). We estimate the level of *gross subsidies* provided by the government per household and the level of *net benefits* enjoyed by the public housing tenant household. The degree of efficiency of the public housing programme can then be calculated. We can also estimate the percentage of households with positive *net benefits*.

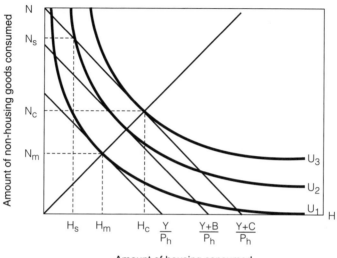

Figure 5.3

**Effect of Public Housing Programme:
Decreases housing consumption
(when $H_s < H_m < H_c$)**

Amount of housing consumed

The effect of the public housing programme on the consumption patterns of current occupants can be studied. We can estimate the gain in housing consumption received by the average household in the public housing programme if the latter were to be replaced by an income supplement equivalent in value to the *gross subsidy*. The percentage of households with positive gains in housing consumption can also be estimated.

Data from the 5% samples of the 1981 and 1991 population censuses are used in our analysis. The detailed estimates are presented in Appendix 2. In our estimation we assume that the ratios of public to market rent are 0.25 and 0.30 for 1981 and 1991. These ratios imply that the market discounts on rental prices of public housing units are 75% and 70%, respectively. Tables 5.1a and 5.1b summarize the main results of these regression estimates.

The estimated *gross subsidy*, *net benefit*, and gain in housing consumption per household will change when the ratio of public to

Table 5.1a

**Gross Subsidy, Net Benefit and Gain in Housing Consumption
by Public to Market Rent Ratio, 1981 and 1991**

	1981			1991		
Public to Market Rent Ratio	0.15	0.25	0.35	0.20	0.30	0.40
Gross subsidy per household	$1,168.4	$742.2	$316.0	$2,579.8	$1,744.6	$909.4
Net benefit per household	$777.6	$436.0	$94.4	$1,940.0	$1,254.3	$568.6
Efficiency ratio (next row ÷ top row)	0.666	0.587	0.299	0.752	0.719	0.625
Gain in housing consumption per household	$458.2	$117.6	–$223.0	$1,033.7	$351.2	–$331.3

Note: 1981 figures are derived from estimates in Wong and Liu (1988); 1991 figures are
         derived from estimates in Wong (1998 forthcoming).

Table 5.1b

**Positive Net Benefits and Positive Gain in Housing Consumption
by Public to Market Rent Ratio, 1981 and 1991**

	1981			1991		
Public to Market Rent Ratio	0.15	0.25	0.35	0.20	0.30	0.40
Percentage of households with positive net benefit	95.6%	84.4%	73.2%	99.3%	94.9%	90.5%
Percentage of households with gain in housing consumption	70.4%	52.0%	33.6%	83.8%	64.5%	45.2%

Note: 1981 figures are derived from estimates in Wong and Liu (1988); 1991 figures are
         derived from estimates in Wong (1998 forthcoming).

market rents is changed. The estimation method we use is designed
to enable us to evaluate the impact of a change in the ratio of public
to market rents on these values. Tables 5.1a and 5.1b also present
estimates on *gross subsidies*, *net benefits*, the gain in housing
consumption, and other related figures. Estimates are also given for
these values when the ratio of public to market rents are changed by
a factor of one-tenth, both upward and downward, from the
assumed ratio prevailing in the years 1981 and 1991. This allows us

to evaluate the effect of increases in public rents and private rents on public housing tenants.

Efficiency Effects

The gap between the *gross subsidy* granted and the *net benefit* received is enormous. The monthly *gross subsidies* provided by the government to the typical household were estimated to be $742.20 in 1981 and $1,744.60 in 1991. However, the average monthly *net benefits* received by the typical household in the public housing programme were only $436.00 in 1981 and $1,254.30 in 1991.

The efficiency of the programme can be assessed with reference to the efficiency ratio defined as the ratio of *net benefit* to *gross subsidy*. A high ratio will imply that a large proportion of the money spent by the government generates benefits valued by the household. An efficient programme will have an efficiency ratio of one.

We found that the efficiency ratio was 58.7% in 1981 and 71.9% in 1991. These two estimates mean that for each dollar the taxpayer spent on the public housing programme in these two years, only 59 cents and 72 cents, respectively, worth of housing services were valued by the tenants, but the remaining 41 cents and 28 cents, respectively, were wasted because of resource misallocation. In other words, an enormous amount of resources were wasted. The efficiency of the programme improved considerably between 1981 and 1991 after the government reduced public housing subsidies by lowering the discount on public sector rents.

The average efficiency loss per household was estimated to be $306.20 ($742.20 – $436.00) a month in 1981 and $490.30 ($1,744.60 – $1,254.30) a month in 1991. The value of the economic efficiency loss to society as a whole can be obtained by multiplying the average value of the loss per household by the number of households in the public housing sector. In 1981 and 1991 there were, respectively, 439,581 and 604,016 households in the public housing programme. This implies that the economic

Table 5.2

**Gross Subsidy Net Benefit per Household and Positive Net Benefit
by Income Brackets, 1981 and 1991**

Income Brackets	1981				1991			
	Gross Subsidy per hh ($)	Net Benefit per hh ($)	Efficiency ratio	Positive Net Benefit (%)	Gross Subsidy per hh ($)	Net Benefit per hh ($)	Efficiency ratio	Positive Net Benefit (%)
Bottom 10%	460	352	0.77	96.72	1,567	1,120	0.71	100.00
2nd 10%	528	385	0.73	93.28	1,621	1,213	0.75	100.00
3rd 10%	579	409	0.71	90.78	1,655	1,262	0.76	99.51
4th 10%	619	427	0.69	88.80	1,688	1,304	0.77	97.88
5th 10%	664	446	0.67	86.61	1,724	1,341	0.78	96.11
6th 10%	713	466	0.65	84.26	1,767	1,376	0.78	93.97
7th 10%	775	491	0.63	81.32	1,820	1,402	0.77	91.27
8th 10%	867	525	0.61	77.06	1,892	1,402	0.74	87.61
9th 10%	1,013	573	0.57	70.52	2,005	1,313	0.65	81.69
Top 10%	1,619	31	0.02	70.20	2,237	(663)	n.a.	66.76

Note: 1981 figures are derived from estimates in Wong and Liu (1988); 1991 figures are
derived from estimates in Wong (1998). "Positive Net Benefit" refers to the percentages
of Hong Kong households that have received net benefit (from housing subsidy).
hh means household. n.a. means not applicable.

efficiency loss to society was $1.62 billion in 1981 and $3.55 billion in 1991. The figures represent 0.95% and 0.53%, respectively, of gross domestic product in their respective years. It is an enormous loss for society to bear year after year.

Although the vast majority of the households obtained positive *net benefits*, this is not the case for every household. Some 15.6% of households in 1981 and 5.1% in 1991 were receiving negative *net benefits*. This is a somewhat puzzling result.[1] Since households have to wait in line for a number of years to obtain a public housing unit, they would not join the programme unless there were positive benefits for doing so. One possible explanation is that although they were getting negative benefits now, they expect them to become positive in the future.

Another explanation is that some of the households that were receiving negative *net benefits* were not living in the unit and that the reported information was deliberately incorrect. These households are likely to be among high-income groups, for which the chance of receiving negative benefits is more likely. This is confirmed by figures in Table 5.2, in which the reported number of households with negative net benefits rises with income levels.

Some 29.8% and 33.24% of the households in the top 10% of the income distribution for the years 1981 and 1991 are worse off under the programme; but only 4.28% and 0% of the households in the lowest 10% of the income distribution for the respective years are worse off. The larger incidence of negative *net benefits* among high-income groups is a result of the fact that they are forced to consume much less housing than they would have wanted to. By contrast, households in the lower-income groups rarely receive negative *net benefits,* because they now consume more housing than they otherwise would.

In general, *gross subsidies* tend to rise with household income. The same is true for *net benefits*, except for households in the top income brackets. We also found that the degree of efficiency was lower in high-income brackets and higher in low-income brackets in 1981. However, the efficiency ratio was quite stable for almost all income groups in 1991, with the exception of those in the top 10% of the income distribution. In general, the direct provision of subsidized rental housing to lower-income households is relatively less inefficient than it is to higher income ones.

The imposition of the double rent policy in 1988 drove out some well-off tenants. Some of those who remained in the programme will be paying double rent. In principle, this will help increase the efficiency of the programme among high-income groups. However, this will not be reflected in our figures, because it is not possible to identify which households in our data are paying double rent. Since all households are assumed to be paying the standard rent, therefore, the measured efficiency ratios of the high-income groups in 1991 are underestimated.

The estimates also imply that *net benefits* would become negative for the typical household if public housing rents were doubled. A doubling of public housing rents would raise the ratio of public to market rents to 50% in 1981 and to 60% in 1991. At these levels, the proportion of public housing tenants with negative *net benefits* will fall to 56.4% in 1981 and 81.7% in 1991. One would expect that few tenants in the high-income groups would have positive *net benefits,* and this is borne out by figures in Table 5.2. It explains why the double rent policy was strongly opposed by most public housing tenants. Even some tenants who are not presently well off would be concerned because they could be affected by the double rent in the future.

Housing Consumption Effects

Would a public housing tenant consume more housing services if the public housing programme were replaced with an income supplement whose value is equal to the *gross subsidy?* The resulting increase in income for the typical household would be equal to the difference between the average value of the *gross subsidy* and the *net benefit.* The amount for 1981 is $306.20 and for 1991 is $490.35.

According to calculations provided in Table 5.1, the income supplement would increase the monthly housing consumption value for an average household by $117.60 in 1981 and $351.17 in 1991. These are very significant increases given the value of the income supplement. The typical household would allocate some 38.4% and 71.6%, respectively, of the increase in income to housing consumption in the years 1981 and 1991. The fact that households are willing to allocate such a large proportion of the increase in income to housing services clearly shows that the existing public housing programme is forcing many households to consume too little housing.

The under-consumption was particularly serious in the more recent of the two years for which we have presented estimates. As incomes rose between 1981 and 1991, the demand for housing also rose. Public housing tenants unfortunately are locked into the same unit and therefore are naturally more prone to under-consumption. The gain in efficiency of the public housing programme we found earlier is due primarily to the increase in the ratio of public to private sector rents rather than to changes in the physical housing consumption bundle.

Most people believe that the public housing programme helps tenants consume more housing services than they otherwise would. According to our calculations, this in clearly not the case for Hong Kong's public housing programme. Our finding here reconfirms the conclusion we describe in Chapter 3, in which we show that the typical public housing unit is about 60% of the size of a private unit (see Table 3.5) but that the income distribution of public and private sector renters are quite similar (see Table 3.4).

We found that 52% and 64.5% of the households in 1981 and 1991, respectively, consume more housing services under the public housing programme than they would have otherwise if they had been given an equivalent income supplement. The inefficiencies of the public housing programme arise chiefly because some families are forced to consume too much housing and some to consume too little.

Under-consumption is most prevalent among high-income groups. In contrast, households in low-income groups are over-consuming housing services. The figures in Table 5.3 confirm these conclusions. We find that 73.87% and 94.09% of the household in the bottom 10% of the income distribution in 1981 and 1991, respectively, had positive gains in housing consumption. For households in the top 10% of the income distribution the respective figures were 37.55% and 0%.

The public housing programme therefore improves the housing consumption of low-income groups but worsens it for high-income groups. Moreover, figures in Table 5.3 also show that the average gain in housing consumption among the top 30% of the income groups in the public housing programme is negative. It is not surprising therefore to expect that households in these income groups with sufficient savings would purchase property in the private sector either for investment purposes or for their own use. A survey conducted by the Housing Authority in 1992 found that at least 74,000 out of 580,000 (or one out of eight) public housing households owned property in the private sector. A follow-up

Table 5.3

Gain in Housing Consumption and Positive Housing Consumption by Income Brackets, 1981 and 1991

Income Brackets	1981		1991	
	Gain in Housing Consumption ($)	Positive Housing Consumption (%)	Gain in Housing Consumption ($)	Positive Housing Consumption (%)
Bottom 10%	473	73.87	1,228	94.09
2nd 10%	397	67.55	991	85.03
3rd 10%	340	62.98	838	79.39
4th 10%	293	59.37	684	73.87
5th 10%	241	55.39	513	67.90
6th 10%	184	51.13	302	60.74
7th 10%	110	45.80	29	51.85
8th 10%	−1	38.13	−356	39.92
9th 10%	−181	26.43	−1,016	21.20
Top 10%	−1,481	37.55	−3,411	0.00

Note: 1981 figures are derived from estimates in Wong and Liu (1988); 1991 figures are derived from estimates in Wong (1998 forthcoming). "Gain in Housing Consumption" refers to estimated dollars gained or lost per household; "Positive Housing Consumption" refers to the percentage of households in the income bracket that have gained in housing consumption.

survey in 1994 found that nearly 90,000 households owned property.[2] In a special check done on 2,250 families within a twelve-month period in 1995, some 500 tenants were discovered subletting their units for profit or using them as storerooms.[3]

The effects of the public housing programme on consumption patterns and the distribution of benefits among public housing tenants have been explored in considerable detail. These two aspects are intimately related to the efficiency and equity aspects of the programme. The gap between subsidies provided and benefits received is a manifestation of the programme's inefficiency. Moreover, empirical results have shown that the programme creates enormous distortions in the consumption patterns of public housing tenants. Poor tenants consume too much housing, and rich tenants consume too little. The statistics we obtained illustrate the extent of the public housing programme's inefficiencies. These inefficiencies are revealed in different aspects of the programme, which will be discussed below.

Manifestations of the Programme's Inefficiencies

The most obvious inefficiency in the public housing programme results from a public housing tenant's severely constrained choices. The Housing Authority assigns a housing unit to a household. Such a unit is tied to a given set of characteristics: appearance, construction materials, environment, neighbourhood amenities, transport facilities, etc. A household has very few options in terms of this assignment: either it accepts the unit as is or turns down the offer and is placed on the waiting-list again. Rather than returning to the queue, tenants usually accept the unit offered because of its low rent because it would be years before they would be offered another chance at a flat. The direct provision of housing produces a misallocation of resources, and the gap between the gross subsidies provided and the benefit received illustrates this waste.

Furthermore, there is a distortion problem in tenant consumption patterns. Gross misallocation occurs at higher income levels. Poor tenants consume too much housing, while rich tenants consume too little, given their household characteristics. The only bright spot in this scenario is that most poor families increase their housing consumption, whereas rich families decrease their housing consumption. While some people may still deem the former to be desirable, justifying the latter seems almost impossible. Subsidizing the rich so that they consume less housing contradicts the purpose of the public housing programme. Moreover, it also deprives the genuinely poor from access to valuable subsidies.

Rich families stay in the programme only because of the low rent. Our results show that the benefits to rich tenants are quite small and can easily be eroded by increases in public housing rents. It appears that a policy that enticed well-off tenants to leave the programme would substantially decrease the level of inefficiency in the existing system and would be defensible on equity grounds, as well. Putting into effect such a policy could create more vacancies in the public housing sector, which would reduce some of the pressure on the government to increase spending on public housing. Rising public housing rents can also indirectly increase the attractiveness of the home-ownership scheme to well-off public housing tenants.

Another equity issue is that of who is admitted into the public housing programme. Families on the waiting list are subjected to a screening process before they can qualify for public housing. Households tend to lie and to disguise their true characteristics in order to be accepted into the programme. For example, during the period prior to the screening process, one of the two working members of the household may cease to work or may work in places where it is difficult to verify employment in order to be eligible for public housing. The inequity created in the system hinders the provision of housing services for families who really need them. To counteract this phenomenon, the government could earmark more resources for fraud prevention. However, this would be costly and would increase government spending. It could also make the programme even more inefficient than it was before.

The poor quality of public housing is another source of waste. Public housing estates were not built under careful specification. They were built using standard designs, and there were cases of pervasive fraud and negligence. Poorly constructed flats are one reason that the recent scheme of privatizing public housing estates has raised concern. Some of the flats have problems with water leakage from the ceilings and plaster coming off the walls. The ability to monitor public housing estates is hindered by government bureaucracy. In the private housing market, if a developer builds poor-quality housing and earns a bad reputation, people will be less willing to pay for the flats. Since public housing is built by the government and provided to tenants at low rent, Housing Department officials have no incentive to maintain the quality of the flats. In exchange for lower rent, tenants have to accept poor-quality housing.

Poor management and maintenance results from the tenants' negligence, as well. Public housing renters are not willing to invest in and maintain their dwellings, since they do not own them. The failure to invest in public housing units stems from insecure property rights. Tenants realize that if the government wanted to, it could take back the property. They could lose it all and would have no court protection.

Evidence from countries like Peru illustrates the importance of recognizing property rights.[4] When a massive influx of immigrants rushed into the urban city of Lima, they erected poorly managed illegal squatters' dwellings, forming slums in the urban area. The government on occasion decided to recognize such squatters. Once they had legal rights and owned the premises where they lived, substantial improvements occurred in the area.

When the numbers of squatters in Hong Kong mushroomed in the late 1940s, the government experienced difficulties in moving them out of the urban periphery. Although these squatters were illegal, once they moved in, they developed a sense of undefined property right to their dwellings. Cases have shown how government decisions to clear squatter areas created tremendous opposition on the part of tenants. The only way to move squatters out was to give them better deals through the resettlement programme and later through the public housing programme. Once the government embarked on such a programme, it found itself caught in an unending task of resettling squatters. The programme encouraged private renters to become squatters in the hope that the government would soon offer them accommodation. The more squatters the government resettled, the more people chose to become squatters. The programme sucked up more and more resources, and inefficiency became entrenched in the public housing programme.

The public housing programme has implications for land-use planning as well. By building huge public housing estates as part of the "New Towns" development, the government has necessitated the planning and co-ordination of a whole array of resources such as clinics, schools, and transport systems. Estate planning has become a form of global planning and may have an enormous impact on the global allocation of resources. Take the town planning of Sha Tin and Fo Tan as an example. The aim of Sha Tin

New Town was to create an integrated residential neighbourhood. Ideally, residents were to work in the industrial area of nearby Fo Tan. This has not happened, however. Sha Tin residents have to commute to the urban area to work every day, and those who actually work in Fo Tan live in the urban area. The inefficiency created by the failure of planning is embodies in the constant traffic jam in the Lion Rock Tunnel, which connects Sha Tin with the urban Kowloon Peninsula. By moving families into new towns, the government has indirectly forced them to make restricted and inefficient choices about where to live, where their children will be educated, what kind of support network they will rely on, etc. These decisions are all tied together when a household moves into a new town. This has generated enormous inefficiencies in society, as it reduces the scope of the market for scarce resources and the households' freedom to choose.

We have demonstrated the inefficiencies generated by the public housing programme based on the data we obtained from economic and statistical analyses. The first step toward improving efficiency in the programme was the Double Rent Policy, which was put into effect in 1986 and which required households whose incomes exceeded twice the Waiting List Income Limit to pay double rent. The idea was to reduce subsidies to well-off tenants and to encourage home ownership. The new proposal of privatizing public housing is a more aggressive step toward improving efficiency. If privatization succeeds, it will cure a lot of the ills we have discussed and will eliminate the programme's inefficiencies.

Notes

1. Part of the explanation may be due to errors in estimation.

2. See *South China Morning Post*, Friday, 7 October 1994.

3. See *South China Morning Post*, Friday, 17 September 1995.

4. See the fascinating study by Hernando de Soto (1992).

CHAPTER 6

The Case for Privatizing Public Housing and Recommendations for Implementation

Summary of Findings

The foregoing chapters have provided a reinterpretation of many commonly held beliefs about public housing in Hong Kong. Some of the results are surprising, but others are not. In my view, the most iconoclastic reinterpretation is that of the origins of the public housing programme. Contrary to popular belief, it was not private developers' inability to cope with the massive influx of immigrants into Hong Kong in the immediate post-war years that had led to the growth of squatter settlements and the eventual implementation of the public housing programme. The Shek Kip Mei fire provided the occasion for introducing the resettlement programme; it was not the reason.

The public housing programme grew out of the failure of government policy to relax planning controls and building standards and to release land in the face of a momentous increase in demand triggered by the influx of immigrants from China. Crowded private tenement living conditions and the emergence of squatter settlements represented the only possible market response under the circumstances. The government worsened matters by imposing rent control in 1945. This made it almost impossible to redevelop private housing, because of the problem of repossessing domestic premises and evicting tenants.

The government had failed to act at the beginning and hoped that the influx of immigrants would be a temporary one. The chaos of the administrative bureaucracy in the immediate post-war years probably contributed to this inaction. Eventually the government was drawn into the process of providing public housing in order to clear squatter settlements to facilitate urban redevelopment. The bureaucratic planning approach to housing was to become a major force in Hong Kong's urban development. Public housing's objective has since changed many times. It has moved from squatter resettlement to provision of low-cost housing for low-income families and subsequently to the provision of home-ownership units for middle-income families.

Except in the early resettlement phase, the public housing programme has generally failed to achieve its stated goals by as much as half of the initial target in terms of delivering the planned number of housing units. The resettlement scheme was most successful because its goals were well defined and straightforward. Nevertheless, it created perverse incentives, as numerous families living in private housing units decided to become squatters in order to be eligible for resettlement. As a consequence, after resettling one million squatters, the government found itself faced with another million awaiting resettlement.

Subsequent public housing schemes were much grander in scale and more ambitious in their objectives. As a result, the government found itself faced with the task of administering very complex pro- grammes with multiple objectives and serving diverse client groups, many of whom were becoming increasingly politicized. It was no longer obvious that the numerous initiatives and measures were mutually consistent. Policies were adopted to remedy the unfore- seen consequences of earlier policies. The attempt to apply both carrot and stick measures to induce well-off tenants to give up their public housing units is a case in point and is primarily a result of decades of neglect in applying any form of means test or asset test.

The public housing programme also failed to meet basic efficiency and equity objectives. Evidence from numerous surveys and census data reveals that there is little difference in the distribution of income between tenant families in public and private housing units.[1] The inefficiency cost of the programme is shockingly high and has resulted in enormously distorted consumption patterns for large sections of the population. We discovered that high-income households consume far too little housing and low-income households consume too much. While the latter may still be thought of as a positive welfare transfer, albeit an inefficient one, it is not at all clear how the former might be defended. One obvious manifestation of the inefficiency of the programme and its distorting effect on housing consumption is the fact that the household income of public and private housing tenants are almost identical, and yet public housing tenants live in units that are only on average 60% of the size of the average private tenant's unit.

These findings point to only one conclusion. There must be a better way to resolve the housing problem.

The Aims of Privatization

The public housing programme has many obvious problems, but can privatization solve all or even most of them? In this section we consider the various objectives toward which privatization should aim. Since housing is intimately connected with almost all aspects of economic, social, and political life, it is necessary to develop the case for privatization from a number of different perspectives. We shall consider the economic benefits, the equity effects, the social impact, the moral dimension, and the political consequences of privatizing public housing. Government bureaucracies have a natural tendency to resist any radical reform measures that may have important consequences for society because of the uncertainty that the measures inevitably carry with them. A policy change of such proportion would also trigger social resistance, since it is inevitable that it would ruffle the feathers of some vested interests. It is, therefore, not enough to simply make a plausible case for privatization. The case must be overwhelming for it to overcome government inertia and public resistance.

Table 6.1

Average Growth Rate of Per Capita Consumption and GDP

	Consumption %	GDP %
1966–1976	4.97	5.26
1976–1986	7.26	5.72
1986–1996	4.95	4.52

Table 6.2

Benefits of Increasing the Per Capita Consumption Growth Rate

	5%	5.5%	6.0%
Per Capita Consumption Growth Rate	5%	5.5%	6.0%
% Increase in Per Capita Consumption	0	9%	16%
Increase in Per Capita Consumption in 1996 (current prices)	0	$10,250	$11,842
Increase in Total Consumption in 1996 (current prices, billion HK$)	0	$64.69	$74.74

Note: The discount rate is 5% and the base level rate of per capita consumption growth rate is 5%.

The Economic Case

The inefficiency of the public housing programme was examined in Chapter 5, and the manifestations of the inefficiency were discussed in Chapter 3. We showed that estimates of the economic inefficiency were approximately 1% and 0.5% of gross domestic product (GDP) in 1981 and 1991, respectively. Wong and Liu (1988) have shown these figures to be lower bound estimates. In other words, the true cost of economic inefficiency to society may be even larger. The 1991 estimates of inefficiency are lower than the 1981 estimates because public housing rents were increased during the interim period so as to narrow the differential between public and private sector rents. Since 1991 private sector rents have risen faster than public sector rents as a consequence of the housing shortage in the private housing sector. It is quite possible that economic inefficiency might have risen somewhat since 1991.

What would the economic cost to society be if the public housing programme were to continue in its present form? The simple answer is that the growth rate of per capita GDP will not be able to realize its potential by approximately an additional 0.5% to 1%. This is a very large sum when compounded into the future. The magnitude of this loss to a typical individual can be evaluated by assuming that the growth rate of per capita consumption will increase at the same rate as the per capita GDP will. Table 6.1 shows the average real per capita growth rates of consumption and GDP for the three periods in the years 1966–96. The growth rates of consumption and GDP are similar in the periods 1966–76 and 1986–96. In the period 1976–86 the growth rate of consumption is higher by about 1.5%.

Let us assume that in the absence of privatization, per capita consumption will rise at an annual rate of 5%. Privatization will therefore increase the growth rate of per capita consumption to between 5.5% to 6%. In Appendix 3 we describe a model for estimating the benefit to an individual of obtaining the higher rate of consumption growth due to privatizing public housing. The results are presented in Table 6.2 assuming a discount rate of 5%.

A higher per capita consumption growth rate due to privatizing public housing would result in an across-the-board increase in per capita consumption of 9% to 16%. This is a very significant gain and amounts to a welfare increase of between $10,250 to $11,842 per capita measured in 1996 Hong Kong dollars.

The aggregate benefit for the economy as a whole would be equal to the product of the population and the per capita gain in consumption. The value of this gain to the economy when evaluated in 1996 HK dollars is equivalent to between $64.5 billion and $74.7 billion. This is a very significant gain.

It should be noted that these estimates do not reflect the full benefits of privatizing public housing, because they only measure static gains. It is highly likely that privatization of the public housing stock would result in dynamic gains for improving capital market imperfections. When public housing is privatized, the units become transferable assets that can be used as collateral for loans. Households would be in a better financial position to start small businesses, which would be of enormous value to Hong Kong's economy, whose foundation is characterized by small and medium-sized family-based businesses. Another way to reduce capital market imperfections is to create more favourable conditions for the development of mortgage loan securitization. For these reasons, as well as for reasons noted earlier, the benefits presented here of privatizing the public housing stock are underestimated.

Distortion of Consumption Patterns

The public housing programme severely constrained the housing choices of eligible tenants. Most households were compelled to consume either too much or too little housing. These distorted housing consumption patterns are the manifestations of the economic inefficiency of the programme.

In Chapter 3 we show that the choice of jobs, the decision to participate in the labour market, the cost of commuting, schooling opportunities for children, and other types of behaviour are also affected by the programme. The housing consumption decision cannot be separated from the consumption of non-housing goods and services. Distortions in the housing market will naturally spill over into the rest of the economy, compounding inefficiency effects.

For this reason, the estimates of economic inefficiency obtained in Chapter 5 will also be understated because they do not take into account the general equilibrium effects of these spillovers.[2] Privatizing public housing will eliminate these distortions. With the emergence of a market for public housing units, tenants will become owner-occupiers and will have an opportunity to trade their units. The market will therefore eliminate these distortions.

Income Distribution Effects

Contrary to popular belief, the public housing programme has not reduced income inequality. Given the complex and changing criteria based on which public housing units are allocated over time, it is not surprising that the assignment of housing units appears both arbitrary and random in its effect on the distribution of income. These arbitrary and random elements should be recognized as a serious injustice. Their continuation will only give rise to further demands from the community to expand and extend government provision of housing benefits.

The privatization of public housing will not in and of itself improve the distribution of income. Indeed, privatization has been criticized by some of its opponents on the grounds that it will provide an additional benefit to public housing tenants who have already enjoyed subsidized housing for many years. What these critics miss is that the failure to privatize will also continue to perpetuate injustice.

The measures adopted by the Housing Authority to encourage public housing tenants to give up their units through easier access to the Home Ownership Scheme (HOS) and the Home Purchase Loan Scheme (HPLS) also provide additional benefits to the public housing tenant. Indeed, from an equity and justice point of view, these measures primarily benefit well-off tenants. Privatization, however, will at the very least provide additional benefits to a much larger group of public housing tenants, and the criteria will not have further regressive income distribution effects.

The process of enticing public housing tenants to give up their public housing units through the carrot of the HOS and HPLS is slow and is limited by the supply of new HOS units and the availability of loanable funds. The unjust situation created by the public housing programme will drag on for a long time.

Maintaining the status quo would accomplish little. Prospective public housing tenants on the waiting list cannot benefit when large numbers of public housing units remain frozen. The sale of public housing units would, however, generate more revenue for the Housing Authority. It would therefore be in a better financial position to expand the HPLS for the benefit of those on the waiting list.

It appears on balance that privatizing public housing would restore justice and prevent the worsening of the regressive income distribution effects more effectively and quickly than adhere to the status quo.

Social Concerns

The most important feature of housing as a freely transferable asset is that it can be a store of value. In Hong Kong property is an important hedge against inflation. In the 1990s it has become the only effective asset with which most people can hedge against the inflationary erosion of savings.

The opening of China and the expansionary migration of manufacturing industries across the border have created an unprecedented economic boom in Hong Kong. Under the linked exchange rate regime, domestic prices, including asset prices, have escalated as demand continues to outpace supply growth. Rising property prices are therefore well supported by economic fundamentals. Nevertheless, the predicament of those without property assets, the retired, the elderly, and those who have lost their jobs is an unhappy one.

The privatization of public housing would provide one-third of the households in Hong Kong with an asset with which to hedge against inflation. This is a highly desirable outcome in a situation where government authorities have few instruments that they can use to curb inflation. It would resolve in one stroke, and at almost no cost to the government, the ills of inflation for most of Hong Kong's have-nots.

Privatization would provide elderly households living in public housing units with a valuable asset, which they could deploy effectively to support their living standards in old age. It could, for example, help them finance an annuity, extract contributions from their children by leaving them a bequest, and perhaps even accommodate relatives in their unit legitimately.

In providing the elderly with an asset for self-support, public welfare expenditure would be saved, dignity in old age would be preserved, and filial piety would receive a boost. The rewards of privatization would mean more than just material benefits for the elderly; it would offer them a more satisfying life in their twilight years — a life over which they could take personal responsibility and control.

The Political Case

Most governments have recognized the benefits of political and social stability based on a community of home-owners. Political philosophers have recognized for centuries the subtle and intimate relationship between the moral foundations of a free society and its underlying property rights structure. No society can be truly free if its inhabitants are overwhelmingly residents of public housing estates. This is particularly so in Hong Kong because housing is extremely expensive and property assets are the most valuable and important asset in the portfolio of most households.

As Hong Kong becomes increasingly democratic and open, it is imperative to reconsider the structure of property rights in our society. A community enslaved by the state will vote in favour of more entitlements, but one composed of free men and women will support greater protection of private property rights and individual freedom. Only in the latter situation can we realize the full benefits of a democratic system, which include the promotion of economic prosperity and social stability and the protection of the freedoms of its citizens.

Planning and the Market

Experience around the world has shown that economic planning has not lived up to its expectations in providing the requisite incentives and institutions for the operation of an efficient economy. Planning appears to function best when the scope and scale of activity is very well and narrowly defined and specific. Economic planning on a grand scale almost always fails in a grand way.

Housing planning in Hong Kong has suffered this fate. The early resettlement programme was probably the only stage at which planning objectives and goals were achieved: to build as quickly as possible large numbers of housing units of a very basic standard at low cost.

Ensuing housing plans were progressively more ambitious, had multiple objectives, aimed to meet the demands of different groups, and produced a variety of housing units of varying quality. As the objectives became more varied and complex, they were often inconsistent with each other when implemented. It is worth noting that the ambitious housing schemes of the assertive governor Murray MacLehose also failed to reach their goals. In the end, only half of the targeted goals were met. It is true that part of the shortfall could be attributed to the unexpectedly difficult conditions created by the two oil shocks in the 1970s. Interestingly this only underscores the pitfalls of concocting grandiose schemes. Experience has shown that markets are often able to weather unforeseen shocks better than the best laid plans.

The Housing Authority's recent strategies to contain the public housing programme, expand home-ownership, entice well-off public housing tenants to give up their tenure, and expand the use of market incentives are laudable. They reveal a thorough understanding of the issues at stake. Unfortunately, the administrative measures that can be taken are necessarily very limiting. The process is painfully slow and is littered with political minefields that often distract attention from the objective and sometimes derail the reform process. Privatization of public housing promises to be the only way to bring about the swift changes that administrative measures have been unable to effect.

Relevant Factors to be Considered

In designing a scheme to privatize public housing, it is necessary to take into account several related issues. The first is the treatment of restrictions on subsequent transfers. The second is the initial sales price of the units. The third is the fact that no privatization scheme can be set without making reference to the existing policies governing the initial sales and subsequent transfers of HOS units. The fourth is the number and selection of units to be privatized. The fifth is the future redevelopment opportunities of public housing estates to be privatized.

On Relaxing Subsequent Transfer Restrictions

Any attempt to privatize public housing units with the purpose of realizing the aims of privatization set out in the previous sections must include removing or relaxing restrictions on subsequent transfers, for otherwise there is little reason to privatize at all.

In Chapters 4 and 5 we show that restrictions on subsequent transfers have important consequences for the value of public housing units to be privatized. Public housing units that cannot be subsequently transferred are much less valuable to prospective buyers. Even if the sitting tenant intends to keep and occupy the acquired unit permanently, the right to transfer the unit freely is still valuable because the plans of the tenant-turned-owner may change in the future.

If one were not able to subsequently transfer privatized public housing units, how much would tenants willingly pay for them? Estimates from Chapter 5 show that the average public housing tenants value their units at only 60% to 70% of the units' market value. The median public housing tenant will probably value the unit at an even lower percentage level. The gap between a household's personal valuation of the worth of the unit it occupies and the unit's market value will vary across households. We have shown that this gap, which is the difference between the gross subsidy and the net benefit, reflects the underlying inefficiency of the public housing programme.

In the presence of severe restrictions on transfers, one would conjecture on the basis of these figures that less than half of the units could be sold if their prices were set at 50% of the market value. This is consistent with the failure of the previous attempt to sell public housing to sitting tenants. The proportion of units in individual public housing estates that could be sold will also vary inversely with the incidence of households with a large gap between gross subsidy and net benefit.

Households in old public housing estates are less likely to buy these units when there are severe transfer restrictions. These households have spent many years living in their estates, and it is far more likely that their current housing preferences are not satisfied by the attributes of the unit they are now living in. Hence, with severe transfer restrictions, old public housing estates could not be successfully sold unless the prices were set at very low levels. One should note that this effect is independent of the quality or age of the unit, because the latter affects only the market value of the unit but not the gap between the household's personal valuation of the unit and its market value.

I conjecture that if a majority of the units in the old public housing estates were to be sold, prices could not be set at more than 25% of the units' market value.[3] If there were no transfer restrictions, then the household's personal valuation of the worth of the unit would coincide with its market value. In that case, a modest discount from market prices would make the units sufficiently attractive to most tenants.

On Pricing of Public Housing Units

A discussion of the sales prices of public housing units is only meaningful if regulations governing subsequent transfers have been determined. In principle, there are three key regulations governing the transfer of public housing units that are worth consideration. They are (1) the length of the holding period before a unit can be transferred, (2) the effective transfer price, net of any payments including land premium that have to be paid to the Housing Authority, and (3) the pool of eligible buyers who can purchase the unit. All of these regulations have the effect of reducing the value that can be obtained by the vendor from transferring the unit.

The more restrictive the regulations, the lower the sales price will have to be. There is clearly a trade-off between restrictive regulations and the sales price. Suppose a unit can be freely sold on the open market, but the vendor is required to repay the full land premium to the Housing Authority. In this case, the vendor would be unwilling to pay more than the replacement cost of the unit. Given that the replacement cost of a typical public housing unit is not very high, I conjecture that the typical public housing unit could only be sold at a nominal price under these circumstances.

Other factors are also relevant in determining the appropriate sales price. The affordability of the unit to the household has been widely cited as an important factor. The size, quality, location, age, and other attributes of the unit are also relevant. But these are technical rather than conceptual matters that need not detain us in this study.

It is worth noting that the relevance of the question of affordability depends on the transfer restrictions in place. If privatized public housing cannot be transferred, then it is important to set a sales price that is relevant to the specific income circumstances of each tenant rather than with reference to the value of the unit he or she is occupying. If privatized public housing units can be freely transferred without any restrictions whatsoever, then sales prices can be set with reference to the value of the unit. What is required is that the sales price be set in such a way that there is an element of subsidy that allows even poor tenants to afford some unit on the market. When a public housing tenant is presented with the option to purchase the unit he is occupying, but finds it too expensive, he can always sell it and buy a unit he can afford. All that is necessary for this transaction to take place is that the net proceeds from the sale of the unit be sufficient for him to afford another unit on the market.

On Convergence with HOS Transfer Regulations

Arrangements for privatizing public housing units and the regulations governing any future transfers cannot be set independently of the regulations for transferring HOS units. Once a public housing unit is privatized, there is no longer any institutional difference between an HOS unit and a public housing unit except for the regulations governing their transfer arrangements. It is therefore highly desirable to have convergence in transfer regulations to avoid making false institutional distinctions between the two types of units.

There are at present a number of key restrictions governing the transfer of HOS units. In the first five years HOS units can only be sold to the Housing Authority at the original purchase price. Unless nominal property prices in the market were to fall and the households were to have a cash flow problem, there is almost no incentive to sell the unit. In the second five years HOS units can be sold to the Housing Authority at a price related to the sales price of new HOS units. This would provide some modest gains if property prices in the market had risen. Both restrictions imply that the Housing Authority is the only legitimate buyer. In other words, the vendor is only permitted to sell the unit to other households that are qualified for the HOS scheme.

After ten years HOS units can be sold on the open market, but the seller must return to the Housing Authority the updated value of the discount on land premium that she received. The typical discount is 50% at the time of initial purchase. The policy of returning to government the discounted land premium will reduce substantially the capital gain that can be obtained from the appreciation of property prices.

A new regulation that effectively reduced the constraining effects of the sales restrictions in the first ten years was recently introduced. The regulation allowed HOS units to be sold to public housing tenants and those on the waiting list after the first three years. The price was to be determined freely in a market comprising a restricted pool of eligible buyers. This new regulation had the effect of expanding the pool of eligible buyers of three- to ten-year-old HOS units to include households that are public housing tenants and those that are qualified for either HOS units or public housing units. After adjusting for size, quality, location, and age factors, the price of the three- to ten-year-old HOS units are likely to closely relate to the price of new HOS units sold by the Housing Authority. The age factor enters the equation in two ways: first, as a vintage effect and, second, as the number of remaining years before the unit can be sold on the open market.

Convergence in the present state implies that privatized public housing units can be sold after three years to existing public housing tenants, former public housing tenants whose units have been privatized, those on the waiting list, occupants of HOS units, and qualified applicants for HOS units. The units can in the three- to ten-year period be sold to the Housing Authority on terms analogous to the new HOS units. These terms would include a 50% discount off the land premium and the replacement cost of the structure.

After ten years privatized public housing units can be sold on the open market, again on terms analogous to the HOS units. In other words, the land premium that is to be returned to the government should reflect a 50% discount. *The relevant number of years referred to here is the year in which the public housing unit was first occupied and not the year in which it was privatized.* Defining the number of years in this manner ensures that public housing units would become convergent with the HOS units. Furthermore, it implies that the majority of the public housing units that are sold can be immediately transferred either on the open market or in the market for public housing units among eligible buyers.

Public housing units that are less than three years old cannot be transferred. Public housing tenants always have the option not to buy the unit and to remain tenants. The rent they pay, excluding the portion attributable to management fees and rates, can be applied toward the purchase price of the unit, should they choose to exercise the right to buy the unit in the future. New public housing units would come under the same set of regulations and arrangements.

A scheme to privatize public housing units that converges with the present regulations for transferring HOS units cannot realize the full benefits of privatization. The benefits would rise if HOS regulations were further relaxed. This could occur in a number of ways. First, the first three-year period could be reduced. Second, the three- to ten-year period could be shortened. Let me note here that the time periods refer to the date when the units were first occupied and not to the date when they were privatized. Third, further discounts on the repayment of land premium to the government is allowed when the units are sold on the open market. Fourth, the sales price of public housing units could be lowered.

From an economic perspective, relaxing the first two of these four regulations would allow society to reap more benefits sooner, and is always desirable. The problem from a regulator's point of view is that speculative profiteering would be encouraged if new HOS units could be resold immediately. This would be most embarrassing for the government. Its effort to help house society's disadvantaged would be seen as doing little more than providing short-term speculative profits for a devious and lucky few.

For this reason, the scope for reducing the first three-year period is quite limited. The three- to ten-year period can, however, be shortened. The case for shortening it to a three- to five-year period would be very strong if no discounts on the payment of land premium to the Housing Authority were allowed when the units were sold on the open market. Without discounts on land premium, most of the capital gains would be returned to the government, and there would be little justification for delaying the efficient circulation of more units on the open market.

In the absence of discounts on land premium it is imperative that the vast majority of public housing units be sold at a nominal price. The issue of whether it is more desirable to have a higher sales price with significant discounts for land premium or a lower sales price with small discounts is debatable. From an economic point of view, they are substitutes. From a political and administrative point of view, it is probably advisable to adopt a low sales price with small discounts. A low sales price makes the privatization scheme politically popular at the time when the units are sold and administratively convenient because there is no need to radically change the existing regulations governing the transfer of HOS units.

On the Scope and Pace of Privatization

Mr. Tung Chee Hwa's first policy address in October 1997 proposed to sell 25,000 units each year over the next ten years. This would in effect privatize almost 40% of the entire public housing stock. I applaud these proposals but am convinced that the scope should be further extended and, more importantly, that the pace of privatization should be accelerated. An active and stable secondary market for ex-public housing units can only emerge when a substantial number of units that are differentiated in terms of their selection are placed on the market. This will result in greater and more immediate efficiency gains and will also seem more equitable.

Consider what happens when only a small number of units are privatized. For simplicity, we assume for the time being that there are no restrictions whatsoever governing these transfers. Units that are privatized can be sold to other public housing households or to those living in the private sector. For many households, the decision to buy another unit is linked to the decision to sell their own unit. Given the available quality and selection of public housing units, it is likely that potential buyers are primarily those living in the public housing sector. Since the buyers and the sellers are largely the same group of households, it is therefore necessary to privatize a large number of public housing units in order to have an active market. Households on the waiting list for public housing can constitute a second group of potential buyers, but their numbers are small compared to the total stock of public housing households. Hence, an active market in privatized public housing units will only emerge when a large number of units with a wide selection are available.

If only a small number of units are available on the market in the beginning, there will be few transactions. The prices that emerge initially may be idiosyncratic. On the supply side, the price will reflect the number and choice of units on the market, and on the demand side it will reflect the preferences of the households whose units have been privatized. If privatization is gradual, with a fixed number of units becoming available each year, then a new batch of suppliers and demanders are introduced onto the market sequentially. Some uncertainty will be generated because the market is not likely to be informed as to the selection of units that will be made available each year, at least not at the outset of the privatization process.

Another important consideration relevant to gradual privatization is the issue of equity. Since market conditions vary from year to year, and individual plans differ across households, the incidence of benefits would depend on when one's own unit was privatized. The question of timing is always important for household welfare. A process of gradual privatization would impose a random element on the welfare gains for all public housing households. Indeed, if early privatization were to result in considerable gains for some households but not for the rest, then privatization would be seen as unfair. This would be most unfortunate. It would be even worse if some of the units were later sold shortly before market prices moved downwards. Public discontent would then be enormous. It would be even more disastrous if the regulators decided to avoid possible public discontent by privatizing public housing in such a way as to obliterate any opportunity for profit making through imposing severe restrictions on subsequent transfers.

An equitable way of privatizing the public housing stock and ensuring an active, stable market in these units requires the privatization process to be completed within a short span of time and to involve as many units as possible. There is no obvious reason for why the units cannot be privatized in one instance.

On equity grounds it may be difficult to justify the privatization of only 40% of the units. In other words, why are some households denied the opportunity to benefit from privatization? It has been suggested that it will be impossible to sell very old units. Even if this is the case, there is no reason not to try. There is of course the concern that if the old units were privatized, it might be difficult to redevelop the block because of the difficulty in reassembling units that have scattered ownership.

A third important consideration relevant to gradual privatization is that public housing tenants are now alerted to the fact that they can reap a windfall gain when they are offered the opportunity to buy their public housing unit. Hence they would put their housing decisions on hold and wait for their turn to be invited to accept the offer. Since the typical tenant does not know when he or she will be called, the vast majority of them will therefore adopt a wait and see decision. This would immediately have a negative impact on the take up of HOS units among public housing tenants.

The new HOS units that are put on the market will have to be taken up mainly by the private housing tenants on the waiting list. This in turn would shorten the waiting time for HOS units and would have a negative knock on effect of private housing demand. Such an effect would be entirely mitigated if there were no or few restrictions on the transfer of privatized public housing units and if most of the units were to be sold immediately and quickly. In this case, the public housing tenants would be able to realize an immediate windfall gain from buying their own units. Wealth would be created in society and this would boost private housing demand as predicted by our analysis in the earlier chapters.

It is important to note therefore the scope and pace of privatization is an important one, for otherwise privatization could achieve a totally opposite set of results. To avoid any incongruity between intentions and consequences the details of the privatization have to be carefully considered.

Facilitating Redevelopment of Privatized Blocks

The difficulties encountered in redeveloping the worst private tenements in the urban areas are well known. The Land Development Corporation was created in 1986 and was endowed with land resumption powers, but there have been only a few successful cases of redevelopment. The land assembly process in the presence of scattered title ownership in multi-storey apartment buildings proved to be an exceptionally difficult task under existing laws.

For this reason, to facilitate urban redevelopment it is necessary to amend various laws and establish new institutions to lower the transactions cost of land assembly. These two ideas were recently endorsed in principle in Mr. Tung Chee Hwa's policy address. In his address he stated that "development is a complex process, but we must address the challenge more rigorously. . . . This will involve a number of measures, including the redevelopment of old industrial areas into housing, a review of plot ratios and set time limits for handling public objections to residential developments."

He further stated that the "ability to resume land for redevelopment is the key. We aim to set up an Urban Renewal

Authority by 1999 to build on the good work that has been accomplished by the Land Development Corporation. We will introduce legislation to give the Authority effective powers to carry out resumption and comprehensive redevelopment. We will also introduce legislation to assist property owners and developers to assemble land so as to quicken the process of renewal by the private sector."

In the presence of these new proposals, one should be much more optimistic about the prospect of redeveloping old public housing estates even if they were privatized. The process of redeveloping privatized public housing estates can be facilitated if a special provision were built into the privatization act. One could, for example, define property rights in privatized public housing units in a block or even several adjacent blocks to be held in a form analogous to shares in a company. Redevelopment would become mandatory if a majority of the shares held by owners voted in its favour.[4] Compensation would be paid to all remaining owners at an agreed-upon rate based on estimates of the market value of the property. A time limit would be set to resolve any disagreements about the estimated value. Third-party adjudication would be introduced and would be binding on all parties if disagreement over the proper amount of compensation to be paid could not be settled within the allotted time period.

Such an arrangement would in fact speed up redevelopment of old public housing estates that have been privatized, because it would allow market forces to determine the pace of redevelopment. If redevelopment were left to the Housing Authority, then a different set of criteria would have to be applied. The pace of redevelopment would depend on the supply of available public housing units to relocate existing tenants and perhaps even the supply of new public housing estates. Very often the process of relocation is very slow because of holdouts and costly administrative negotiations that are sometimes highly politicized. In my view the market solution is less coercive and more efficient than the bureaucratic one is. One should note also that provisions that facilitate the redevelopment of old blocks would actually enhance the value of the units when they were privatized. It is therefore desirable to privatize even old public housing estates under these circumstances. This would be highly beneficial for society because many of these units are located in valuable core urban areas.

One of the drawbacks of this proposal is to create a class of old public housing estates, whose property rights structure is different from private tenement blocks. As a consequence, it encourages the development of former old public housing estates at the expense of the private blocks. This is not necessarily an undesirable outcome given that the old public sector units are probably more in need of redevelopment than the old private sector units. Nevertheless, a better solution would be for the government to adopt more effective legislation to speed up the redevelopment of old estates that would apply equally to all units. From the point of view of efficient resource allocation it would not be desirable to leave the task of redevelopment of old public housing estates to the Housing Authority.

Determining the Sales Price

The determination of the sales price of privatized units is a controversial and complex task. The market value of a unit comprises two components. The first component is the replacement cost of the structure. The second component is the market value of the land. Under current arrangements applicable to the sale of Home Ownership units, 50% of the land premium is paid to government at the time of the sale and 50% is fully subsidized when the units are first released. Owners who subsequently sell the HOS units on the open market return to the government the updated value of the fully subsidized portion of the land premium.

By analogy, if these same pricing arrangements apply to the privatized public housing units then owners who subsequently sell the units on the open market should return to the government only the updated value of the fully subsidized portion of the land premium. The implied sales price of the units to be privatized would be set at a level that equals the replacement cost of the structure plus

50% of the value of the land premium at the time of the sale. The price of the unit will then vary with the age, quality, and location of the estate, and other specific attributes of the unit within the estate.

To determine all these factors will be a mammoth task. As a simplifying assumption and a workable benchmark I propose to use the present discounted value of the rental payments of the public housing units as the sales price. This replaces the implied sales price described in the previous paragraph, i.e., the replacement cost of the structure plus 50% of the value of the land premium. The appropriate period over which the rental payments should be discounted for tenants in the public housing programme should be close to infinity. The age of the unit is not important, because the public housing entitlement is almost a permanent one. The age of the unit may be taken into account to a certain degree because with privatization a permanent entitlement is exchanged for a marketable unit whose value depends partly on its age, but this is a technical policy issue that is secondary to the discussions and proposals advanced here.

An operational definition of the appropriate time horizon can be between ten and thirty years. The discount rate to be used is 5% and is the same as that used earlier to discount future consumption. In Table 6.3 we give examples of the estimated sales price for public housing units that are charging different rents. We distinguish between three levels of rents: high monthly rents of $2,500, medium monthly rents of $1,500, and low monthly rents of $500. These rents in real terms are assumed to rise at a rate similar to the rate of growth of per capita real consumption. For illustrative purpose we use a growth rate of 5%.

As is to be expected, the present value of future rent payments depends on the period over which it is discounted. At the end of the day the choice of what price to set is a political issue, but there are some economic considerations.

In my view, if transfer restrictions are based on the proposals outlined in points 3 and 4 of this section (pp. 107–113), then the sales price should be based on the present discounted value of future rents over a 20-year to 30-year horizon. This would represent approximately a 30% to 40% discount on the market value.[5] For the

Table 6.3
Present Discounted Value of Public Housing Rental Payments

Current Monthly Rent	Present Value (Years = 10)	Present Value (Years = 20)	Present Value (Years = 30)
Low = 500	60,000	120,000	180,000
Medium = 1,500	180,000	360,000	540,000
High = 2,500	300,000	600,000	900,000

Note: The discount rate and the future rental real growth rate are both assumed to be 5%.

units in the old blocks it would also be important to make provisions to facilitate subsequent redevelopment as proposed in point 5 of this section (pp. 113–115). My reason for choosing a 20-year to 30-year horizon is quite simple; it will ensure an overwhelming take up rate. When the units are finally sold on the free market, the typical household would have some room for capturing the capital gains associated with the appreciation of land values. However, not all households would be able to benefit equally because the underlying preferences and characteristics of the households and the unit they occupy may have considerable variation.

A high sales price based on the present discounted value of future rents over a longer horizon will be justified if the government agrees to discount the land premium that has to be returned to the Housing Authority when the units are sold on the open market. Unfortunately, this approach has three drawbacks. First, the issue of affordability may become relevant for some households because some units cannot be sold immediately on the open market. Second, the problem of convergence with HOS transfer restrictions will be compromised. Third, households with high discount rates may be unwilling to pay the high sales price, and this will reduce the success rate of the privatization scheme.

Arranging Financial Assistance for Tenants

Public housing units that are sold to the tenants will have to be financed. Traditionally banks are the main source of mortgage loans. There is no reason why banks would not accept public housing units as acceptable collateral if they can be transferred. The units are sold at substantial discount therefore the loan to equity ratio would be very favourable. The only outstanding question is whether the banks have sufficient funding to finance the sale of large numbers of public housing units over a short period of time. It will no doubt require some innovative financial arrangements.

Fortunately, Hong Kong has recently established the Hong Kong Mortgage Corporation Limited. This will be an appropriate vehicle for providing such arrangements. Given the large number of public housing units that can be privatized this would also make it possible to create a significant market for trading mortgage backed securities. Such a development would not only make it possible to privatize public housing units on a large scale, but also help the development of the capital market in Hong Kong.

Housing Authority Policies on New Units and Unsold Units

The Housing Authority will continue to build new housing units. These units can be either for rental or for purchase. Rental units can be bought any time after three years in accordance with the provisions and subject to the same conditions we have discussed earlier. The distinction between ownership units and rental units will be determined entirely by the tenure arrangements and will not be based on the physical block to which the unit belongs.

We recognize that not all units can and will be sold. The Housing Authority will continue to act as the landlord for tenants in the unsold units. Over time these units are likely to be relatively few in number, and it is entirely possible that the Authority will play the role of a minority shareowner in many blocks.

Summary of Recommendations

The main policy recommendations of the present study are listed below.

1. Permit all public housing units that are at least three years old to be privatized immediately and as quickly as possible. Gradual privatization must be avoided.

2. Relax transfer restrictions and ensure that they converge with those that apply to Home Ownership Scheme units.

3. Revise transfer restrictions on all privatized public housing units and Home Ownership Scheme units to allow all units that are three years old to be transferred at market-determined prices among ex-public housing tenants and applicants for public housing units on the waiting list.

4. Revise transfer restrictions on all privatized public housing units and Home Ownership Scheme units to allow all units that are five years old to be transferred on the open market at market-determined prices. The updated value of the subsidized portion of the land premium should be returned to the government. The subsidized portion is typically 50% of the market value for both public housing and Home Ownership Scheme units.

5. The sales price of the privatized units should be set at a level roughly equal to the present discounted value of future rental payments over a 20-year to 30-year period.

6. The implied sales prices for the units with different levels of rents are given on page 121.[6] It should be emphasized that these are for illustrative purposes and could be further refined to take into account other relevant factors.

7. Public housing units that are privatized could be subject to the provision that the property rights in these units are analogous to the shares of a company. This provision may be necessary to facilitate future redevelopment of these

units after titles have become scattered through privatization.

8. Financing the sale of public housing units can be facilitated
   through the use of mortgage backed securities through the
   recently established Hong Kong Mortgage Corporation
   Limited. This would also help the development of the
   capital market.

9. All new housing units built by the Housing Authority
   should be available either for sale or rent. After three years
   tenants should be permitted to purchase units that are
   rented.

10. The present timing is ideal for privatizing public housing.
    At a time when Asia is moving into an economic recession,
    Hong Kong's low consumption spending would benefit
    enormously from the economic stimulus of privatization.

Notes

1. This contradicts the findings by Hsia and Chau (1978) and Lin (1985). Both studies are based on faulty analysis that assumes the result rather than proving it.

2. See discussion in Wong and Liu (1988), pp. 1–20.

3. A more precise estimate could be obtained using the methodology we had previously developed with more detailed data available with the Census and Statistics Department and the Housing Authority.

4. The majority rule used here could be a simply majority, a two-thirds majority, or some other variation. The ease of development would vary inversely with the size of the majority. In principle, the optimal rule would be to allow redevelopment to occur at a pace commensurate with the growth of demand. The rule once established should not be changed to avoid volatility in the rate of redevelopment.

5. A numerical example for calculating the percentage discount from market value is provided in the following chapter.

6.

Current Rent	Proposed Sales Price 20 Years Period	Proposed Sales Price 30 Years Period
$500	$120,000	$180,000
$1,500	$360,000	$540,000
$2,500	$600,000	$900,000

CHAPTER 7

Epilogue

On Monday, 8 December 1997 the Housing Authority proposed a Tenants Purchase Scheme (TPS) to sell public housing units to sitting tenants.[1] The proposal was similar in many ways to the recommendations proposed in the previous chapter with a few key exceptions, which are worth highlighting here.

First, the proposal favoured a programme to sell gradually part of its public housing stock. The Housing Authority's TPS proposed to sell only 250,000 units over a 10-year period.

Second, the proposal imposed restrictions on resale of privatized public housing units that did not fully converge with those governing HOS units. The Housing Authority proposed that both HOS and TPS units could be transferred to the Authority at the original price in the first two years or at the prevailing TPS price in the third to fifth year from first assignment. Resale of both HOS and TPS units was allowed (1) to eligible persons and other tenants in the secondary market after two years from first assignment and (2) freely in the open market after five years from first assignment subject to payment of a premium proportionate to the original discount. The problem here is that unlike the HOS units, the date of first assignment of the TPS units defines the date when ownership is transferred to the tenant but not when occupancy of the unit first took place. What it means is that almost all the TPS units that are sold today could not be immediately transferred.

Third, the implicit discount of the TPS units proposed by the Housing Authority based on what they call the "adjusted replacement cost" approach is not very different from my proposal to set

Table 7.1

Comparison of Housing Authority's Proposal and My Proposal

	Housing Authority's Proposal		My Proposal	
(1) Market value of unit	$1,800,000	$1,800,000	$1,800,000	$1,800,000
(2) Monthly rent of unit	$1,500	$1,500	$1,500	$1,500
(3) Calculation of sales price	Equals 12% of market value calculated as a 60% special first-year discount on 30% of the estimated market value of the unit		Equals present value of future public housing rents over a fixed period of:	
			20 years	30 years
(4) Sales price	$216,000	$216,000	$360,000	$540,000
(5) Proposed original discount at first assignment	30%	40%	50%	50%
(6) Payment to government of premium proportionate to original discount upon transfer of the unit on the open market	$1,260,000	$1,080,000	$900,000	$900,000
(7) Effective discount[1]	18%	28%	30%	20%

Note: [1] (Row 1 – Row 4 – Row 6) / Row 1.

the sales price with reference to the present discounted value of expected future public housing rents. Consider a unit whose current market value is $1.8 million and on which the tenant has to pay a monthly rent of $1,500. The Housing Authority's proposed sales price is 30% of the assessed market value, but there is a further provision to offer a special credit of 60% if the buyer purchases the unit in the first year. This effectively lowers the sales price to 12% of the assessed market value, i.e., $216,000. The Housing Authority proposes that when the unit is subsequently resold on the open market the owner has to return to the government 70% of the estimated market value of the unit. The discount that is provided by the TPS is in effect 18%.

Under my proposal the sales price depends on the period over which future rents are discounted. The sales prices are $360,000 over a 20-years period and $540,000 over a 30-years period. They are, respectively, 20% and 30% of the assessed market value of the unit. Under my proposal when the unit is subsequently resold on the open market the owner has to return to the government 50% of the estimated market value of the unit. The discount that is provided in my proposal is 30% if the sales price is set at a level equal to the present value of 20 years of discounted future rents and is 20% if the period over which rents are discounted is extended to 30 years.

For a diagrammatic comparison between the Housing Authority's proposal and my proposal see Table 7.1. Clearly the 18% discount provided by the Housing Authority's TPS proposal is very similar to the 20% discount under my proposed sales price based on the present value of future rents discounted over a 30-years period. The main differences between the two approaches are that the sales price under my proposal can be more easily calculated and will be far less dependent on property market conditions. The latter factor became very pronounced as property market conditions corrected rapidly in the wake of the financial crisis in Asia that happened at about the same time when the Tenant Purchase Scheme was announced. The Housing Authority was compelled to lower the amount that has to be returned to the government after the unit is resold on the open market from 70% to 60% the estimated market value of the unit. The effective discount that is provided by the TPS was therefore increased from 18% to 28%.[2]

The financial crisis in Asia also amplified the negative knock-on effects of the TPS proposal. The fact that the privatized units could not be transferred immediately and the gradual process of privatization led to an immediate dampening effect on the demand for private housing. In principle, as we have shown in the main body of this study, the privatization of public housing should be a process of wealth creation that would increase the size of the housing market and also result in a net increase in housing demand. But as with all complex policy proposals, the devil is in the details. Nevertheless there is no reason to disparage the Housing Authority's bold proposal to privatize public housing. It is a decision that is long overdue and should be welcomed and applauded. Indeed the popularity of the proposal with tenants and the high take-up rate show conclusively that privatization is the right policy choice. The details of the implementation can be easily improved even at this stage and the public should focus on making the necessary amendments in the upcoming review of the Tenant Purchase Scheme so that the full benefits of privatization can be realized.

Notes

1. See Hong Kong Housing Authority (1997b). The recommendations contained in this study were publicly released on Friday, 5 December 1997.

2. The disadvantage of setting sales price with reference to volatile property market conditions is that an element of arbitrariness is introduced into the equation that has implications for fairness. One may of course view the flexibility of the Housing Authority's TPS proposal as an advantage rather than as a disadvantage. If this is the case such flexibility is also present in my proposal through varying the time period over which the present value of future rents are discounted.

Appendix 1

Major Events

1940s

1945   On October 22, rent control was imposed on all existing pre-war private premises under the Proclamation of 1945.

1947   The Landlord and Tenant Ordinance was enacted on May 23, to replace the Proclamation of 1945, setting controls on the rent increase of all pre-war private dwellings to 30% of the standard rent. The standard rent was defined as the rent payable for the unfurnished premises on or most recently before 25 December 1941.

1950s

1950   Population increased from 600,000 persons in 1945 to 2.1 million in 1950 due to the massive influx of refugees and returning residents at the War.

1951   The government approved squatters in certain tolerated areas.

1951   The Hong Kong Housing Society was established to provide homes for middle-income families.

1953   Following a disastrous fire in a squatter settlement in Shek Kip Mei in December, the government initiated the building of basic resettlement accommodation with the object of clearing land occupied by squatters.

1954   An increase of 55% of standard rent for all pre-war domestic premises was allowed.

1954   Eight six-storey buildings — the Mark Is — were built over the ashes of the Shek Kip Mei squatter settlement, providing basic but permanent accommodation for the former squatters.

1954   The Hong Kong Housing Authority was formed with operations similar to those of the Housing Society.

1955   On August 17, the Landlord and Tenant Ordinance was amended. Henceforth, the Tenancy Tribunal was effectively granted the power of eminent domain in reconstruction proposals and to determine the rate structure of compensation. The cost of evicting tenants was greatly reduced.

1955   The Buildings Ordinance was changed through new regulations introduced in 1956 to permit much more intense land use.

1960s

1962   New regulations were introduced to scale down the plot ratios and site coverage in order to alleviate the over development that followed the relaxation of the Building Ordinance in 1956; the regulation was effective in 1966.

1962–1966   This was a grace period; a wave of private residential development, most of which was concentrated in the old inner suburbs, took place.

1963   Rent Increases (Domestic premises) Control Ordinance was enacted to control increases in rent of post-war domestic premises. The Ordinance was allowed to expire in 1966.

1963   A working party was set up to examine the squatter and resettlement situation. The swelling tide of squatters, which sterilized large areas of land, made this necessary.

1964   The government issued a White Paper entitled "Review of Policies for Squatter Control, Resettlement and Government Low-Cost Housing", in which a ten-year programme to build 1.9 million resettlement units and 290,000 government low-cost housing units were announced.

1967   The government provided 32,000 public housing flats.

1968   The Landlord and Tenant Ordinance was further amended to permit landlords to negotiate directly with their tenants for a surrender or termination of their tenancy in return for compensation.

1970s

1970   In June, The Rent Increases Control Ordinance was enacted, covering the majority of tenancies and sub-tenancies in post-war domestic premises completed or substantially rebuilt after 16 August 1945.

1971   The total share of public sector housing was 52.1% — more than the private sector's share, which stood at 47.9%.

1972   The regulations controlling pre-war and post-war premises were consolidated into legislation in the Landlord and Tenant (Consolidation) Ordinance.

1972   In October the government under the Governor Murray MacLehose formulated a ten-year housing programme that aimed to provide public housing for 1.5 million persons from 1973 to 1983.

1973   In April a restructured Housing Authority was set up to co-ordinate the provision of all public housing (excluding those flats built by the Housing Society).

1976   The Home Ownership Scheme (HOS) and the Private Sector Participation Scheme (PSPS) were introduced.

1979   Legislation was passed to exclude rent controls on tenancies in pre-war buildings for business purposes to take effect on 1 July 1984.

1980s

1980   An amendment was adopted to permit self-use as a legitimate ground for possession of domestic premises. This change favoured landlords over sitting tenants in repossessing rented domestic premises.

1980   The Middle-Income Housing Scheme was introduced as an extension of the Private Sector Participation Scheme but was discontinued in 1982 since private housing prices were affordable at that time.

| 1981 | Legislation was amended to provide for permitted rent for domestic premises to be eight times the standard rent and in subsequent years the legislation was amended each year to raise the permitted rent. |

1981   In September the value of land was excluded from flat prices under the PSPS and MIHS, since flat prices would otherwise have been too high for the target groups.

1984   The Housing Authority issued a consultative document, "A Review of Public Housing Allocation Policies".

1985   The Housing Authority issued the "Green Paper on Housing Subsidy to Tenants of Public Housing".

1987   The government announced its Long-Term Housing Strategy in April.

1988   In April the Hong Kong Housing Authority was reorganized and given a separate financial identity and autonomy together with sufficient flexibility to implement the Government's Long-Term Housing Strategy.

1988   The Home Purchase Loan Scheme was introduced in April to assist households eligible to purchase public sector home ownership scheme flats in buying flats in the private sector.

1988   Also in April the double rent policy was implemented for those who had been living in public rental housing for ten years or more and whose household incomes exceeded the Subsidy Income Limits.

1990s

1991   The Sale of Flats to Sitting Tenants Scheme (SFSTS) was launched in August but failed.

1992   The Landlord and Tenant (Consolidation) (Amendment) Bill proposed to eliminate rent controls by 1994.

1992   In the middle of the year the Housing Authority decided that vacated flats would be improved to a new enhanced standard before they were re-let.

1992	The Rent Assistance Scheme was implemented to grant temporary rent relief to tenants who encountered difficulties.
1992	In December a pilot exercise of the Option to Rent or Buy Scheme (ORBS), a scheme under SFSTS, was launched. A rental-type block in an estate due for rental allocation would be designated for sale and upgraded accordingly. Any flats unsold in the ORBS block would be included in the following main phase of HOS sales, and it was decided that only green form applicants would be allowed to buy the unsold flats. The pilot exercise met with a lackluster response.
1993	The Landlord and Tenant (Consolidation) (Amendment) Bill was amended in July to delay the phasing out of rent control until the end of 1996.
1993	In April the double rent policy was amended. Tenants who had lived in public rental housing for more than ten years and had incomes between two to three times the WLILs were required to pay 1.5 times the net rent plus rates and those with incomes exceeding three times the WLILs would need to pay double net rent plus rates.
1993	A revised Sale of Flats to Sitting Tenants Scheme (SFSTS) was launched but also failed.
1993	The mid-term review on the Long-Term Housing Strategy took place in the summer.
1993	In August an interim loan scheme, called the Sandwich Class Housing Scheme, was implemented for middle-income families.
1994	In May new financial arrangements between the government and the Housing Authority were made. The new arrangements aimed at enabling the Authority to make better use of its surplus cash to speed up the construction of public housing. The Authority would keep the Development Fund. The Authority also set up an Improvement Account within its Capital Works Fund.
1995	In April flat selection commence for Tivoli Garden in Tsing Yi, the first project under the Sandwich Class Program.

1995   The Housing Branch started to review the Long-Term Housing
              Strategy in November. The aim was to take stock of the present
              situation and to formulate a comprehensive strategy to meet
              housing demand well into the next century.

1996   In early 1996 the Home Ownership Committee completed a
              comprehensive review of the HOS, which reaffirmed promo-
              tion of home ownership as one of the Authority's main
              objectives in the coming years. The review recommended a new
              resale restriction regime, a secondary market for HOS flats,
              and measures to promote home ownership among households
              affected by the Comprehensive Redevelopment Programme.

1996   In December it became permissible for flats that had been under
              the HOS for five years to be sold to the Housing Authority; flats
              that had been under the HOS for ten years could be freely sold
              on the market.

1996   In December a resolution was passed to further extend the
              period of phasing out of rent controls to 31 December 1998.

1997   The Long-Term Housing Strategy Review Consultative Docu-
              ment was released in January. The document iterated several
              principles including: augmenting the flat supply, maximizing
              the contribution of the private sector, encouraging increased
              home ownership, and providing public rental housing for those
              in genuine need.

1997   In May the government accepted the Housing Authority's
              proposal to allow a flat that had been under the HOS for three
              years to be sold to the Housing Authority. Previously only flats
              that had been under the HOS for five years could be sold to the
              Authority.

1997   A secondary market for HOS housing units that had been
              occupied for 3 years was permitted to operate in June for
              eligible buyers.

1997   In July the Director of the Planning and Environmental Branch
              announced the plan of land sale for the next twenty-one
              months.

1997

In his policy address on 8 October, the Chief Executive announced the government's commitment to building more public housing. It was estimated that by the year 2000 there would be 141,500 units of public housing built (including rental housing, HOS, PSPS, and sandwich class housing). The target is to build on average 85,000 units, approximately 35,000 private and 50,000 public housing units each year. In ten years 70% of the total population will have their own purchased homes. In addition, the new-home starter loan scheme will help 30,000 families (6,000 a year) who are first-time homebuyers to purchase their own homes. Each family will receive a loan of $600,000.

1997

In December, the Housing Authority proposed a new Tenants Purchase Scheme (TPS) to sitting tenants in line with the recommendations announced by the Chief Executive's Policy Address. The Scheme proved enormously popular although there were criticisms that it had a negative knock on effect on private sector housing prices.

Appendix 2

Ordinary Least Square Regressions of Net Benefit, Gross Subsidy, and Housing Consumption for 1981

	Net Benefit		Gross Subsidy	Housing Consumption	
	Value	p Value	Value	Value	p Value
Intercept	436.0	0.844	742.2	117.6	0.520
	(85.2)	(350.2)	(122.1)	(21.7)	(168.5)
Household income	50.9	−0.051	99.0	−108.9	−0.094
	(18.6)	(39.7)	(30.4)	(37.5)	(56.7)
Household income^2	−1.64	0.00057	0.070	−1.32	0.00128
	(23.2)	(18.9)	(0.8)	(17.7)	(30.2)
Age of head	15.3	0.007	13.3	16.5	0.003
	(7.3)	(6.8)	(5.3)	(7.4)	(2.5)
Age of head^2	−0.168	−0.00006	−0.177	−0.167	−0.00002
	(7.7)	(5.5)	(6.8)	(7.3)	(1.7)
Household size	63.9	0.043	46.8	79.2	0.054
	(7.3)	(10.5)	(4.5)	(8.6)	(10.3)
Household size^2	−4.51	−0.00076	−4.40	1.83	0.00067
	(5.7)	(2.04)	(4.7)	(2.2)	(1.4)
Public to market rent ratio (10%)	−341.6	−0.112	−426.2	−340.6	−0.184
	(74.7)	(51.9)	(78.4)	(70.4)	(66.7)
R^2	0.26	0.21	0.32	0.37	0.31
Cases	4500	4500	4500	4500	4500

Source: Results reproduced from Wong and Liu (1988).
Note: Absolute t-values in parentheses.

135

Ordinary Least Square Regressions of Net Benefit, Gross Subsidy, and Housing Consumption for 1991

	Net Benefit		Gross Subsidy	Housing Consumption	
	Value	p Value	Value	Value	p Value
Intercept	1254.30	0.95	1744.65	351.17	0.65
	(317.30)	(1330.57)	(725.08)	(103.14)	(467.88)
Household income	50.82	−0.012	24.31	−101.61	−0.041
	(65.00)	(82.64)	(51.04)	(150.76)	(149.46)
Household income^2	−1.68	0.000031	−0.11	−0.38	0.000195
	(259.12)	(26.25)	(27.93)	(67.53)	(86.051)
Age of head	13.85	0.0056	5.09	32.01	0.00585
	(6.18)	13.80	(3.733)	(16.59)	(7.491)
Age of head^2	−0.13	−0.000044	−0.055	−0.19	−0.000019
	(5.81)	(11.19)	(4.14)	(10.16)	(2.49)
Household size	359.10	0.048	278.74	14.90	0.0159
	(39.71)	(29.39)	(50.64)	(1.91)	(5.052)
Household size^2	−24.67	−0.0031	−14.93	33.98	0.0068
	(24.16)	(16.57)	(24.03)	(38.64)	(18.975)
Public to market rent ratio (10%)	−685.72	0.044	−835.2	−682.46	−0.193
	(141.63)	(49.99)	(283.42)	(163.66)	(114.31)
R^2	0.62	0.13	0.55	0.61	0.32
Cases	27376	27376	27376	27376	27376

Note: Absolute t-values in parentheses.

Appendix 3

Modelling the Economic Value of an Increase in the Growth Rate of Consumption

A typical household will consume a collection c_t of goods at date t, between dates zero and t, and will evaluate an entire sequence, or process, $\{c_t\}$ of consumption according to a utility function such as (1):

$$E\left\{ \sum_{t=0}^{\infty} \beta^t U(c_t) \right\} \tag{1}$$

If we are to evaluate policies normatively according to their effects on households' welfare as measured by (1), we must be able to determine how different policies will induce different consumption sequences $\{c_{it}\}$ for each household i in this economy.

At the simplest level, let us identify c_t with real consumption at date t, and specialize preferences to:

$$E\left\{ \sum_{t=0}^{\infty} \beta^t \frac{1}{1-\sigma} (c_t^{1-\sigma} - 1) \right\} \tag{2}$$

where β is a constant discount factor with $0 < \beta < 1$ and $\sigma > 0$ is the constant coefficient of relative risk-aversion.

Since we are interested in households' attitudes toward growth, it will be useful to work with a consumption stream with a 'trend' component, such as:

$$c_t = (1 + \lambda) + (1 + \mu)^t, \text{ for } t = 0, 1, \ldots \tag{3}$$

Setting the parameter λ is just a matter of units that will be used later on to provide 'compensation' for variations in the parameters μ. For Hong Kong, the annual growth rate in total consumption is about 5%, so $\mu = 0.05$ can serve as a benchmark value. Thus we may take (3) with $(\lambda, \mu) = (0, 0.05)$ as a rough description of the consumption behaviour the average household is used to and can examine its attitudes toward changes.

Given any choice of (λ, μ) we could simply calculate the value of (2) under the consumption behaviour (3) and call the indirect utility function so defined $U(\lambda, \mu)$. But we will obtain a measure that is easier to think about if we use compensating variations in λ to evaluate various μ changes. To evaluate changes in the growth rate μ, for example, let us define $f(\mu, \mu_0)$ by:

$$U\left(f(\mu, \mu_0), \mu, \sigma_z^2\right) = U\left(0, \mu_0, \sigma_z^2\right) \tag{4}$$

so that $f(\mu, \mu_0)$ is the percentage change in consumption, uniform across all dates and values of the shocks, required to leave the consumer indifferent between the growth rates μ and μ_0. A direct calculation gives:

$$f(\mu, \mu_0) = \left(\frac{1+\mu_0}{1+\mu}\right)^{\beta/(1-\beta)} - 1$$

Given below is a table of this function f, which I will call simply the benefit of increased growth, for $\beta = 0.95$ and a base growth rate of $\mu_0 = 0.05$.

At the parameters used in Table 1, then, consumers would acquire a 16% across-the-board consumption increase as a consequence of an increase in the consumption growth rate from 0.05 to 0.055, and would obtain a 24% across-the-board increase in consumption if the growth rate increased from 0.05 to 0.06. The welfare consequences of 'small' changes are enormous.

Table 1
Benefit of Increased Growth from $\mu_0 = 0.05$ when $\beta = 0.95$

μ value	$f(\mu, \mu_0)$
0.050	0.00
0.055	0.09
0.060	0.16
0.066	0.24

Bibliography

1. Aaron, H. J., and G. M. von Furstenberg (1971). "The Inefficiency of Transfers in Kind: The Case of Housing Assistance," *Western Economic Journal* 9, No. 2 (June): 184–191.

2. Akerlof, George A. (1978). "The Economics of Tagging as Applied to Optimal Income Tax, Welfare Programmes, and Manpower Planning," *American Economic Review* 68, No. 6 (March) : 8–19.

3. Bray, D. C. (1952). Statistical Analysis of Squatter Data, mimeograph, Hong Kong: Social Welfare Office.

4. Castells, Manuel, L. Goh and R. Y. W. Kwok (1990). *The Shek Kip Mei Syndrome: Economic Development and Public Housing in Hong Kong and Singapore*. London: Pion.

5. Census and Statistics Department, Hong Kong (1996a). *Hong Kong Annual Digest of Statistics 1996*. Hong Kong: Census and Statistics Department, Hong Kong.

6. _____ (1996b). *By-census Summary Report*. Hong Kong: Census and Statistics Department, Hong Kong.

7. _____ (various years). *Hong Kong Population Census*, Hong Kong: Census and Statistics Department, Hong Kong.

8. _____ (1976). *Hong Kong 1976 Population By-census*. Hong Kong: Census and Statistics Department, Hong Kong.

9. Chan, Kwok Leung (1986). "Demographic Setting of Hong Kong: Developments and Implications," in Alex Y. H. Kwan and David K. K. Chan, eds., *Hong Kong Society: A Reader*. Hong Kong: Writers' and Publishers' Cooperative, pp. 11–44.

10. Cheung, Steven N. S. (1979). "Rent Control and Housing Reconstruction: The Postwar Experience of Prewar Premises in Hong Kong," *The Journal of Law and Economics* 22, No. 1 (April): 27–53.

11. Clemmer, R. B. (1984). "Measuring Welfare Effects of In Kind Transfers," *Journal Urban Economic* 15 (April): 46–65.

12. DeSalvo, J. S. (1971). "A Methodology for Evaluating Housing Program," *Journal Regional Science* 11 (August): 173–185.

13. De Soto, Hernando (1989). *The Other Path — The Invisible Revolution in the Third World*. New York: Harper & Row Publishers Inc.

14. Drakakis-Smith, D. W. (1973). *Housing Provision in Metropolitan Hong Kong*. Hong Kong: Centre of Asian Studies, The University of Hong Kong.

15. _____ (1979). *High Society: Housing Provision in Metropolitan Hong Kong 1954–1979: A Jubilee Critique*. Hong Kong: Centre of Asian Studies, The University of Hong Kong.

16. Hambro, E. (1955). *The Problem of Chinese Refugees in Hong Kong*. Leyden: Sijthoff.

17. Ho, Lok Sang (1995). "Privatisation of Public Housing: An Analysis of Proposals and a Suggested Alternatives," *Contemporary Economic Policy* 13, No. 3 (July 19): 53–63,

18. _____ (1988). "Towards an Optimal Public Housing Policy," *Urban Studies* 25, No. 3 (June): 204–211.

19. Hong Kong Government (1964). *Review of Policies for Squatter Control, Resettlement and Government Low Cost Housing*. Hong Kong: Government Printer.

20. _____ (1987). *Long Term Housing Strategy — A Policy Statement*. Hong Kong: Government Printer.

21. Hong Kong Hansard (1955), 2 March, p. 40.

22. _____ (1947), 3 July, pp. 191–206.

23. Hong Kong Housing Authority (1984). *A Review of Public Housing Allocation Policies*. Hong Kong: Hong Kong Housing Authority .

24. _____ (1985). *Report to Housing Authority on Public Consultation: Green Paper on Housing Subsidy to Tenants of Public Housing*. Hong Kong: Hong Kong Housing Authority.

25. _____ (1986). *Report of the Committee on Housing Subsidy to Tenants of Public Housing*. Hong Kong: Hong Kong Housing Authority.

26. _____ (1986). *Report of the Domestic Rent Policy Review Committee*. Hong Kong: Hong Kong Housing Authority.

27. _____ (1990). *Report of the Housing Authority's Ad Hoc Committee on Sale of Flats to Sitting Tenants*. Hong Kong: Hong Kong Housing Authority, p. 18.

28. Hong Kong Housing Authority (1993). *A Report on the Mid-term Review*. Hong Kong: Hong Kong Housing Authority.

29. _____ (1997a). *Homes for Hong Kong People: The Way Forward, Long Term Housing Strategy Review Consultation Document*. Hong Kong: Hong Kong Housing Authority.

30. _____ (1997b). *Memorandum for the Housing Authority: Tenants Purchase Scheme*. Hong Kong: Hong Kong Housing Authority.

31. Hopkins, Keith (1971). "Housing the Poor," in Keith Hopkins, ed., *Hong Kong: the Industrial Colony*. Hong Kong: Oxford University Press, pp. 271–335.

32. Hsia, Ronald, and Lawrence L. C. Chau (1978). *Industrialisation, Employment and Income Distribution*. London: Croom Helm.

33. Johnson, Sheila K. (1966). "Hong Kong's Resettled Squatters: A Statistical Analysis," *Asian Survey* 6, No.11: 643–656.

34. Kehl, F. (1981). "John Stuart Mill's Other Island: Squatters, Real Estate and Hong Kong Government Policy," unpublished paper presented at the 1981 conference of the American Anthropological Association.

35. Lin, Tzong Biau (1985). "Growth, Equity and Income Distribution Policies in Hong Kong," *Developing Economics* 23, No. 4 (December): 391–413.

36. Lui, T. L. (1984). "Urban Protest in Hong Kong: A Sociological Study of Housing Conflicts," M. Phil. dissertation, Department of Sociology, The University of Hong Kong.

37. Maunder, W. F. and E. F. Sczepanik (1957). "Hong Kong Housing Survey 1957," *The Final Report of the Special Committee on Housing 1956–1958*. Hong Kong: The University of Hong Kong Press.

38. Maunder, W. F. (1969). *Hong Kong Urban Rents and Housing*. Hong Kong: Hong Kong University Press.

39. Olsen, Edgar and David Barton (1983). "The Benefits and Costs of Public Housing in New York City." *Journal of Public Economics* 20: 299–332.

40. Ordinances of Hong Kong (1980), *Landlord and Tenant (Consolidation) Ordinance*, No. 6.

41. Pryor, E. G. (1983). *Housing in Hong Kong*, 2nd edition. Hong Kong: Oxford University Press.

42. Siu, Alan K. F. (1990). "On the Privatisation of Public Housing." *HKCER Letters* 5 (November): 4, 8.

43. _____, Y. C. Richard Wong and Liu, Pak Wai (1996). "Inflation in Hong Kong," unpublished manuscript. School of Economics and Finance, The University of Hong Kong.

44. Smart, Alan (1992). *Making Room: Squatter Clearance in Hong Kong.* Hong Kong: Centre of Asian Studies, The University of Hong Kong.

45. Wong, Y. C. Richard and Liu, Pak Wai (1988). "The Distribution of Benefits among Public Housing Tenants in Hong Kong and Related Policy Issues," *Journal of Urban Economics* 23, No. 1: 1–20.

46. _____ and S. Staley (1992). "Housing and Land," *The Other Hong Kong Report 1992*. Edited by J. Y. S. Cheng and P. C. K. Kwong. Hong Kong: Chinese University Press, pp. 309–350.

47. _____ (1990), "The Housing Problem — A New Perspective," *HKCER Letters* 3 (July): 1–2.

48. _____ (1992a). "Privatise Public Housing," Lunch Talk, Hong Kong Centre for Economic Research, Hong Kong, June 3.

49. _____ (1992b). "Building a Better Housing Market," *The Asian Wall Street Journal*, July 30.

50. _____ (1992c). "Privatise Public Housing," *HKCER Letters* 16 (September): 3–4.

51. _____ (1992d). "Privatise Public Housing," *Conference on Residential Housing in Hong Kong*, December 19, Hong Kong, 15 pages. Co-organised by the Department of Business Studies, Hong Kong Polytechnic and the Department of Economics, Chinese University of Hong Kong.

52. _____ (1998). "The Economic Inefficiency of Public Housing in Hong Kong: 1976–1996," unpublished manuscript, School of Economics and Finance, The University of Hong Kong.

53. _____, Alan K. F. Siu, and P. W. Liu (1994). *Demand for Private Residential Housing in Hong Kong*. Hong Kong: Hong Kong Centre for Economic Research.

54. World Bank, The (1993). "The East Asian Miracle: Economic Growth and Public Policy," *A World Bank Policy Research Report*. New York: Oxford University Press.

55. Yeh, A. G. O. (1990). "Unfair Housing Subsidy and Public Housing in Hong Kong," *Environment and Planning, Series C: Government and Policy* 8: 439–454.

56. Yeung, Yue Man and D. W. Drakakis-Smith (1982). "Public Housing in the City States of Hong Kong and Singapore," in John L. Taylor and David G. Williams, eds., *Urban Planning Practice in Developing Countries*. Oxford: Pergamon Press, pp. 217–238.

Index

About the Author

Yue-Chim Richard Wong was born in China, grew up in Hong Kong, and studied economics at the University of Chicago (A. B. 1974, A. M. 1974, and Ph.D. 1981). He is Professor of Economics and Director of the School of Business at the University of Hong Kong. He was Visiting Scholar at the National Opinion Research Center, University of Chicago (1985) and the Hoover Institution, Stanford University (1989). He has been a member of the Mont Pelerin Society since 1992.

He is also Director of the Hong Kong Centre for Economic Research, member of the Economic Advisory Committee (1992–), Hong Kong Committee of the Pacific Economic Co-operation Council (1992–), University Grants Committee (1993–), Steering Group on Health Care Financing (1997–), Hong Kong Housing Authority (1998–), Services Promotion Strategy Group (1998–), and Chief Executive's Commission on Innovation and Technology (1998–).

He served as member of the Working Party on Sixth Form Education of the Education Department (1988–89), Dental Council of Hong Kong (1991–94), Working Group on Institutional Arrangements for the Lantau Port Peninsula of the Port Development Board (1992–93), Industry and Technology Development Council (1993–96), Consultative Group on Services Promotion to the Financial Secretary (1995–96), Finance Committee of the Hong Kong Housing Authority (1996–98), and as part-time member of the Central Policy Unit (1991–92).

His published books include *The Other Hong Kong Report 1990* (co-editor, Chinese University Press, 1990), *The Economics and Financing of Education in Hong Kong* (co-editor, Chinese University Press, 1992), *The Fifth Dragon: Emergence of the Pearl River Delta* (co-author, Addison Wesley, 1995) and *Port Facilities and Container Handling Services* (co-author, City University of Hong Kong Press, 1997). His main research interests are the economics of human resources and the application of economic analysis to public policy. His current research focuses are the public housing and property markets in Hong Kong and the political economy of laissez faire.

The Hong Kong Economic Policy Studies Series

Titles	Authors
❏ Efficient Transport Policy	Timothy D. HAU Stephen CHING
❏ Competition in Energy	Pun-Lee LAM
❏ Privatizing Water and Sewage Services	Pun-Lee LAM Yue-Cheong CHAN

Immigration and Human Resources

❏ Labour Market in a Dynamic Economy	Wing SUEN William CHAN
❏ Immigration and the Economy of Hong Kong	Kit Chun LAM Pak Wai LIU
❏ Youth, Society and the Economy	Rosanna WONG Paul CHAN

Housing and Land

❏ The Private Residential Market	Alan K. F. SIU
❏ On Privatizing Public Housing	Yue-Chim Richard WONG
❏ Housing Policy for the 21st Century: Homes for All	Rosanna WONG
❏ Financial and Property Markets: Interactions Between the Mainland and Hong Kong	Pui-King LAU
❏ Town Planning in Hong Kong: A Critical Review	Lawrence Wai-Chung LAI

Social Issues

❏ Retirement Protection: A Plan for Hong Kong	Francis T. LUI
❏ Income Inequality and Economic Development	Hon-Kwong LUI
❏ Health Care Delivery and Financing: A Model for Reform	Lok Sang HO
❏ Economics of Crime and Punishment	Siu Fai LEUNG